Tainted Love

A Novel

By Madeline Hampton & Jamie Rockymore

Toledo,Ohio|Baltimore, Maryland

www.createspace.com

Tainted Love

ISBN- 13 : 978-0615971926

ISBN- 10 : 061597192X

 This book is a book of fiction. Names,events and places are of the author's imagination. For questions on bulk orders, please contact:

CreateSpace
4900 LaCross Road
North Charleston, SC 29406

Cover Design: Madeline Hampton& Jamie Rockymore. Editing-Madeline Hampton & Jamie Rockymore.

Cover Photos: ©Allen Penton - Fotolia.com & ©Elnenyo,©Missing 35mm &©Purmar- iStock.com

Acknowledgements

First and foremost, I would like to thank God for giving me this vision and putting the right people in my path to accomplish my dreams. I like to thank my readers for supporting my novels and encouraging with your awesome comments and reviews. My parents taught me to never give up on your dreams and God taught me how to be patient. I want to thank my family for their support and close friends. Nothing is impossible when you put God first.

~Author Jamie Rockymore~

Acknowledgements

Father God, I want to thank you for bestowing the gift of writing upon me. In you all things are possible and it's because of you, I am.
For my mother Sheila Marie Huff, may you peacefully R.I.H. and Tonya Smith Moore.

****

To my father, Johnnie Huff Jr. As I said before, you are my rock. You continue to give me such love and support. I love you.You are truly the BEST. To my brother, John Huff, you're my baby and always will be. Stay strong, genuine and caring. Never let anyone take that away from you. To my husband Johnnie Hampton Jr. you are my forever best friend, my heaven sent soul mate. You really do mean the world to me. To Nikki Barnett, you have been right on time for whatever I've needed recently and I can't sing your praises enough. You rock! To Jamie Rockymore who has shown her exceptional talent for writing in this novel. I'm so thankful for the chance to have written with you. This has been one amazing journey. Thank you to my family and friends who have always encouraged me to put my best foot forward. Truly, from the bottom of my heart, thanks to all of you. To everyone who picks up this book and decides to purchase it, thank you because you are helping me fulfill my dream of writing full time. Thanks for helping me chase down my dream and letting it soar through the skies.

Thank you and God Bless.
~Madeline Hampton~

Prologue

Mom told me what guy to look for once I grew older. Her ideas and our conversations about my husband always made me smile. I valued momma's opinion, she was my best friend and til this day I go to her for any advice.

I remember each morning when she'd comb my thick kinky hair on the porch. That was our time to bond and for her a way of telling me what she'd wanted from me, often times we discussed school, but often times we talked about boys. I cherish those moments. I'll never get those days back, that's why they're important to me.

I want you to marry a fine young man; he has to have goals you know? Momma said. *I don't want my daughter dating anyone who's up to no good.* She'd warn me. I'd sit and listen, slightly nodding my head and taking every word in.

I believe everyone is destined to love. It's important and a great feeling. I have yet been introduced to a companion to love. Sure I experienced being loved by my parents. My father showed me how a man is to treat his woman, but that's different love. I want real love, and I decided to stay pure until God showed me the man I need to love.

I never had a boyfriend, not even in school. My friends were a different story. Dating in high school was the thing to do. With nothing else to do besides watching limited television, my friends spent time over each other's house gossiping. As we became seniors in high school I noticed the damages of what love did. My friend Kayla thought she was in love when she became pregnant with Quinton. She freaked when saw her boyfriend hugged up with another woman. After getting into a fight with Quinton's new girlfriend, Kayla spent a numerous amount of time over my house crying and being depressed. That turned me away from love. I didn't want to feel unhappy at such a young age.

Now that I'm older and mature I'm ready for love but I don't know when my timing is going to be right. All I know is what momma and poppa taught me. I'm tired of drawing my own conclusions. I want to feel *real* love from a man for myself.

My momma told me when she met poppa it was love at first sight. He worked at the car wash up the street from her house. When she noticed him walk out to dry Mr. Ray's Lincoln, she knew he was the one. He was tall dark and handsome with a cleft chin. Momma was fascinated. I really don't need fascination. I wanted substance. I want honesty and truth. I want depth and stability but I'll probably wind up with no one because I'm too picky.

I should be more like to my older sister Cassie. She got married at twenty and pregnant before she turned twenty- one. She remained pure for her husband too. I heard poppa say that a man loves when his woman is pure. I want the same thing but when? Some of these boys are handsome but some are fickle too. Momma said if a man ain't trying to make a dollar out of fifteen cents he's fickle.

I saw a cute boy the other day after choir rehearsal. He wasn't real tall but he winked at me. I wondered if he was attracted to a bunch of girls or just a few. Was he similar to me and didn't know who to be fond of, or what to look for? I don't want to resemble Kayla and get depressed and sad over no negro. I admire the white girls on the TV. I want my boyfriend to call and take me to the picture show.

I craved to see the new movie Superfly. I hear that movie is bad. I have some money saved up; tickets are four dollars. I better save my money. I'm not spending my money by taking a boy to the picture show. He better save his money to take me. Maybe that's wrong. I'll never get a man that way. Momma taught me not be stingy when it comes to treating a man. The next woman won't be. I suppose that's true.

Cassie said sparks are supposed to fly and I'm supposed to feel butterflies in my stomach. She felt that with Derrick. I want to feel that. I think I'm ready for the next step. I want to *experience* love. I'm no different than everybody else.

Chapter 1

Shasta Brown took out a rolling pin and prepared to make the dumplings to complete her meal, her plan was to make the chicken and then add the dumplings. She had the onions, green peppers and peas sitting on the counter in a white bowl. She wiped her brow. It was burning up in the kitchen. The raggedy ceiling fan above her spun around, circulating hot air, and the clinking noise from the ceiling fan didn't make it any better.

The air conditioning was out yet again but that was fine. They couldn't afford the cooling bill any way. The window was cracked and a cool breeze did sweep in every now and again. She opened the oven, ready to face more heat in the kitchen.

The cornbread was turning a golden brown, just right. The green beans and collard greens were simmering. The candied yams still had a ways to go but the smothered pork chops were finished. The potato salad was chilling in the refrigerator as well as the enormous chef salad. She rolled the dough and cut it into thick strips and floured them before dropping them into the piping hot pot on the stove. She repeated this action a few dozen times before taking a quick water break.

She rolled out the dough over and over again, cutting the dough into strips and dropping them in the hot pot. She added the onions, peppers and peas and some Lawry's seasoning salt, a dash of pepper and some table salt. The dumplings were beginning to rise now and were looking good. She checked the yams and took the cornbread out of the oven. Everything was about ready to go. She went to the phone on the wall in the kitchen and dialed Laquenta phone number. It was time to go the park. She looked at the red clock above the refrigerator. It read 12:36pm. She wiped her brow again, lucky for her; she had been up since a quarter to 8 cooking.

Thankfully she washed and cleaned the greens the night before otherwise she'd really be behind. Cassie was supposed to be on dessert detail. She had opted out this time but now wished she hadn't. Cassie made two pound cakes and peach cobbler. She probably was sitting back kicking up her heels right now. She looked at the clock again.

It was 12:47pm. Laquenta was on her way, arriving at any minute. She took the yams out of the oven and quickly took down the foil from the overhead cabinet. She wrapped up as much as possible when she heard a knock at the door. She tossed her apron and it landed on the dining room table. She moved to the door and looked out the peep hole. She smiled and opened the door wide.

"Sister Girl, the smell of heaven is in here! You smell nice too but I can't wait til we get to that park."

"You smell good too. What you got on girl?"

"It's called *Outlast.* It's new."

"Wow, it sure smells nice. You bring your food with you or is Neil bringing it later?"

"It's out in the car. I got 6 slabs of ribs, fried chicken, fried okra, smoke neck bones and potatoes." She sighed, "red beans and rice, and of course macaroni and cheese." The look on her face said that she was exhausted, but excited at the same time, the same way Shasta felt.

"Well, I'm ready. Are we gonna have to bring this all out ourselves?"

"Now you know Vindella ain't raising Charlie up right. He's not gonna come help us. We better head to the place to set up." Laquenta stated. Charlie was big kid Laquenta was watching. She usually watched Charlie for extra money on the weekends. His mother didn't care to teach him about becoming a gentleman and without a hands-on father, he's wasn't going to know how to be. Laquenta tried to tell Charlie what women wanted out of a man, but teaching Charlie these important matters were rather complicated.

The ladies got their food together and took it in Laquenta's 1963 green Pinto. It was barely enough room to put Shasta's food in the trunk. Charlie had to hold the cornbread, yams, pork chops and green beans.

He wasn't too happy about that, and even managed to yelp when Laquenta hit a pothole. Shasta secretly laughed. It served him right. He was 5'11 and 210 lbs, an enormous kid. The ladies shouldn't have had to carry the containers themselves, while he sat in the car resembling a mini version of Jack in The Beanstalk. Laquenta was gonna fix that though. Once arriving to the park, Charlie was gonna unload the food and she meant every last dish.

Each time Shasta got time to daydream, she thought about falling in love. She admired gathering with friends and doing things together when the money allowed her to but being alone was what she despised and hated most. She had some awesome friends so there wasn't much time to think about being lonely.

Laquenta made it her business that Charlie used his muscles. It made no sense for someone to be that big and be lazy. Shasta placed the checkered red and white table cloth on two picnic tables located under a huge tree. Laquenta brought her matching blanket too. The ladies were well prepared bringing four blankets, two for the food and two for them to sit on and enjoy their meals.

"How much longer is it going to be before Neil comes? Is he bringing anyone?" Shasta asked, thinking about the food made her mouth salivate. She watched as all the others ate at their designated picnic tables. A few guys were throwing a football, and other guys were playing basketball. Today was a good day to be outdoors. The air was fresh and everyone and their momma was outside this afternoon.

"You full of questions aren't you? I think he's on his way. He told me around 1:30 and it's a little after but he should be here shortly."

"I hope so. I've been slaving over this meal all day and I want to eat before it gets cold." Shasta put the last touches on her food. She made sure the pans were sitting in a good position. She didn't want them to fall over or spill. She placed a large wooden spoon in each dish.

"It's about time." Laquenta shouted as she noticed Neil getting out the car. He was full of smiles as his friend looked around the park. Shasta eyes met his and couldn't believe he was walking towards her. He was something out of a picture show that's for certain. He was gorgeous. Eating lunch with them was going to be hard because she already had a hard time taking her eyes of him.

Shasta watched Neil and his friend greet their friends. The two boys sat down and conversed with a few other white friends before making their way to her and Laquenta. Shasta kept her eyes on Neil's friend. She tried being discrete and managed to eat her food and talk to a few of her and Laquenta's mutual friends, but every few minutes she was eyeing Neil's friend and watching his every move.

Chapter 2

Laquenta waved her hand in front of Shasta's face a few times to get her attention. Shasta nodded and looked away from Neil's handsome friend, who stood in front of her. He wasn't as tall as Charlie but had warm green eyes. His brown hair was short and Shasta liked the way it draped across his right eye. He was athletically built. His strong arms appealed to Shasta. He stood by Neil and looked directly at her. Neil kissed Laquenta on the cheek and made the introductions.

"Sorry, I was late…I had to pick up my partner here, and you know I had to make my rounds and talk to a few friends." Neil said, looking back; he wanted to make sure he wasn't being watched talking with Laquenta and Shasta. "Laquenta, Shasta, this is Seth Avery. His daddy owns the car wash on Telegraph." Shasta nodded. That's where she'd seen him before. It was for a brief moment a few weeks ago but she remembered he was drying cars. His hair was completely different and he wore a baseball cap but she remembered his face, he was too handsome to forget.

Seth immediately stuck out his hand and Shasta didn't hesitate taking it. Their fingers lingered for a few moments longer than necessary before Seth took Laquenta's hand in a firm handshake. Laquenta moved closer to Neil and he instantly wrapped his arm around her waist. Laquenta watched Shasta but she had her head down. She touched her shoulder and Shasta lifted her head but her gaze automatically collided with Seth.

"If Neil was late, I'm to blame. I was still at the car wash until thirty minutes ago. My dad runs a tight ship." Seth didn't elaborate any further, but Shasta sensed he wanted to elaborate. She didn't have time to think about it long because more of their friends arrived and everyone was talking all at once. "We gotta go. Am I going to meet up with you later?" Neil asked. Laquenta nodded her head and Shasta and Seth continued to stare at each other. Neil nudged Seth, snapping him back into reality. Shasta smiled when she noticed what Neil was doing. "I'll see you later as well." Seth said. Shasta continued to smile as she watched the boys walked off.

Neil and Seth were playing catch with some of the younger children and Laquenta talked with Vindella about Charlie. Shasta sat alone at the picnic table. She thought about Laquenta and Neil. He showed Laquenta affection often whenever the time was appropriate. This picnic wasn't the time, but it was obvious she was thinking about him and vice versa. She envied them. She envied the couple feeding the birds holding hands. Everyone appeared happy. Why couldn't she be too? It was a question she asked herself day after day and night after night. Did love have the ability to find *her* or was it just for everyone else?

She was occupied in her thoughts and didn't hear Seth sit down next to her. Her eyes were closed and she inhaled. She smelled soap. She opened her eyes and Seth was sitting next to her. She smiled inwardly and shifted on the bench. She was nervous but didn't want him to know it.

"You were deep in thought, I didn't want to disturb you but I really needed to sit down. I've been up since 6 a.m." Seth said and Shasta thought back to what he had said earlier about his father running a tight ship. *Did his father even know he was here now?*

"Uhh... are you supposed to be at work?" She really didn't know why she was asking but she loved to listen to his distinctive voice. She didn't want him to get in trouble but she was glad he came.

"Actually I am supposed to be at work until three. My dad doesn't know I left. He's hunting with his friends and won't be back until seven. I gave my twelve year old cousin five dollars to finish up at the car wash for me. My dad won't know I left." Shasta listened to him but had to wonder about his father not finding out. Parents always find out what you want to remain a secret...always.

Shasta watched Laquenta and Neil making up for lost time after the others left the park. She envied how open Laquenta was. She never had a care in the world about she was viewed. Shasta on the other hand always wanted acceptance.

"So what are your hobbies?" Seth smoothed his shorts out with his hands.

"Cooking, it relieves the stress," she smiled nervously. "When I get a chance I try to go to the picture show. I don't go often, but when I do, I enjoy it." Shasta looked at the ground. She couldn't imagine looking into Seth's eyes. She was too nervous.

"Would you go with me to the picture show?" Seth asked. He wanted to ask her as soon as he got the chance to talk to her alone. He had been playing basketball with the other guys but once he noticed Shasta alone, he knew his opportunity had come.

"You want to take me…to the picture show?" Shasta asked, wanting confirmation. "Me out of all the girls here in this park?"

"Yes…you, I want to take you out to the picture show. I want to spend time with you…you know, get to know you." Seth placed his elbows on his knees staring at Shasta waiting for an answer. He looked at Shasta as if she was Diana Ross singing on stage.

Shasta became tongue tied, and a bit speechless. *He wants to go out with me?* "That's great. When do you want to go." She asked.

"How about next weekend, my father won't need me at the shop. I know I'll have some free time. You want to meet me at the show or come pick you up?"

"Let's meet," she replied.

"Okay, that sounds great...now don't flake out on me," Seth smiled. Seth's smile was worth a million dollars to Shasta.

"Hey Seth com' on and play...we need another player," a friend of Seth's shouted. Seth got up and looked at Shasta; he winked at her before he joined his friends. Although the sun was beaming and her face was drenched with sweat, Shasta felt warm and cuddly inside.

Chapter 3

After the picnic, Shasta decided to have Laquenta over for some girl talk. She barely had any time to talk with Laquenta during the picnic because both their minds were occupied by the fellas.

Shasta heard Laquenta talking to her mother. Mrs. Brown became accustomed to Laquenta coming over , so she told her to go straight upstairs to Shasta's bedroom. Shasta heard the footsteps getting louder as Laquenta approached her bedroom door.

"Hey sweetie." Laquenta said dressed all in black as if she was coming from a funeral instead of church service.

"Hey lady...how was church?" Shasta asked, she pulled a chair out for Laquenta to sit in as she sat back on her bed. She placed a pillow in front of herself as she crossed her legs.

"Church was awesome if you ask me, although I don't understand why Pastor Samuel always has to yell at the end."

"Oh don't you just hate that?" Shasta giggled.

"Oh girl yes I do! The choir was good; I stood up singing and clapping my hands. I wish we had a drummer boy. I feel like we're back in slavery days clapping with no music, singing hymns." Laquenta pulled her bushy hair back into a pony tail. "Why weren't you in church this morning?" She asked with an attitude.

"Oh, momma was sick. She coughed all this morning. I walked to the corner store and got her a bottle of cough medicine instead of driving there. I needed to think, besides the pleasant breeze was satisfying this morning. Anyways, Momma is feeling better."

"Oh I see." The conversation went into dead silence. Shasta fiddled with what she wanted to talk to Laquenta about. She didn't tell her Seth asked her to the picture show, yet she needed to let her know to catch a ride with her. "What's the matter?" Laquenta noticed how uptight Shasta appeared to be.

"Well...I talked with Seth yesterday,"

"Yes." Laquenta said sitting on the edge of her seat. Shasta got up and made sure the door was locked. She didn't want anyone coming in on their conversation. Shasta's sister was downstairs making sure momma was okay, but Cassie was nosey and she'd make her way upstairs in eavesdrop on their conversation.

"He wants to take me to the picture show," Shasta covered her mouth and giggled.

"That's nice, are you going to go?" Laquenta asked wide eyed.

"Yes...but there's an issue. I can't take the car and go to the show. I'm going to need a ride. I don't want momma questioning me about who I am going with and what not. If you pick me up then she'll assume I'm going with you." Shasta explained.

"That's fine. I'll call Neil and join you two."

"How do you manage to do that?"

"Do what," Laquenta asked looking dumbfounded.

"Talk to Neil, flirt with him, and have not a care in the world who sees you." Shasta asked leaning against the wall behind her bed.

"I'm attracted to him. My momma doesn't know yet, but oh well. We care for each other despite our skin color."

"Yeah, that's how I feel about Seth, but I haven't spent any time with him. How do you spend time with Neil?"

"When we go out, we're always hanging out with a group of friends, so it's not noticeable. But that's about to change. "

"How so?"

"Neil and I have been going out with a group of folks for over six months. I'm tired of it. You know how stressful that is calling friends just to hang out...with a guy?"

"That sounds frustrating. I know you called me a few times to hang out before. Yesterday was the first time I was able to enjoy a day off. If I wasn't working at the discount store, I would've gone to more of your functions. I'm sorry."

"Oh it's not your fault. A girl's gotta make money too. I just want to spend time with Neil and nobody else, is that hard to ask nowadays?"

"Truthfully...yes." Shasta said disappointedly.

"Why can't I just walk down the street and hold Neil's hand? Do you know how many stares and gasps I'd get? I try hard not to care, and at this moment I'm reaching my breaking point."

Shasta nodded her head as Laquenta continued to ramble on about interracial couples. She hated where this world was at this time in their lives. Laquenta had a few black guys in her life she dated, but she wasn't interested in them now. Was that bad on her part? Shasta wasn't sure of the result of spending time with Seth, but she wasn't going to hesitate and pass up a date with someone she admired.

****

"I got your number from Neil, is that okay?" Shasta picked up the phone on the second ring, careful not to disturb her mother resting on the couch. She didn't know who was calling and almost dropped the phone when she realized it was Seth. She felt giddy and the butterflies were soaring wildly in her stomach. She hadn't thought he would call so soon but now that he had, now what? She took a deep breath and tried to calm her racing heart. "It's okay. I didn't think...I well, I'm glad you called." She sighed her relief. That response wasn't bad? She sounded okay, right? Her voice had come out squeaky though. Maybe Seth hadn't noticed.

"I saw Neil after work and asked him to give me your number. He didn't have it of course but got it from Ms. Peters. Do you work with her niece Emily at the discount store?" Seth asked and Shasta nodded, then realized Seth couldn't see her through the phone.

"Yes, I do work with Emily. I'm surprised that Ms. Peters..." Shasta didn't finish her sentence not to sound racial to Seth but Ms. Peters was a huge racist. She always frowned and stared at Shasta whenever she dropped Emily off and picked her up. A few weeks back, she overheard Ms. Peters discussing her and called her that little nigger girl. Why would Ms. Peters give Neil her number?

"You're surprised that Ms. Peters gave Neil your number? She didn't know it was for me. I don't know what excuse Neil gave, he never mentioned me. I swear."

"It's okay. It doesn't matter how you got my number but I'm glad you called." Shasta smiled but heard her momma stirring and realized she had been talking too loud. Once she was sure momma had fallen back to sleep, she sat down at the kitchen table and crossed her legs at her ankles.

"I thought about the two of us going to the picture show last night. I dreamt this silly dream about the two of us watching Lady Sings the Blues. You were Diana Ross and I..."

"You were Billy Dee Williams. Wow." Shasta was stunned. Did he really like black movies or did he think he had to say that because she was black? She had never really thought of what picture to see. She'd love to see that picture show but he had to want to see it too. He did say he had a silly dream about it. Maybe it was silly because it was a black picture show.

"I was Billy Dee. I was handsome and strong and in my dream, you thought the world of me." Seth said and Shasta melted. She clutched the phone cord tight. Her mother began to stir again on the couch and moaned. Shasta knew she should look in on her. She didn't want the conversation to end but knew she had to go. She stood up from her seat at the dining room table and whispered five words into the phone. “Call me tomorrow at seven.” She hung up then before she said something foolish but knew in her heart of hearts that happiness was just around the corner.

Chapter 4

Shasta and Emily walked into the discount store for work. Shasta's shift began an hour after Emily's. Since Emily needed a ride she didn't mind going in early. She figured she'd sit in the break room and reminisce on the short conversation she had with Seth.

She couldn't stop thinking about Seth, she was still surprised he called her last night. She couldn't wait for evening to come, anticipating Seth's phone call. She knew exactly where she was going to be come seven o'clock. She was also going to make sure momma was not by the phone. Around then momma was tired from working and cooking dinner. Shasta talked on the phone with Laquenta every night anyway so momma won't think there was any strange activity going on.

"Have fun in the break room and thanks again for picking me up." Emily mentioned as she put on her work apron. She swiped her card at the time clock and reported to the floor. Shasta dreaded the six hour shift that was ahead of her. She'd rather spent time with Seth, or go to the car wash just to see him.

"Nice to see you here early," Ms. Peters commented as she strolled into the break room. She was the supervisor for Shasta and Emily. No matter how ugly Ms. Peters appeared to Shasta she always kept a smile on her face.

"Good afternoon Ms. Peters, yes I am here early, but that's alright. I have forty minutes until my shift. I'll wait patiently."

"Of course. I'd tell you to clock in now but I don't think that'll be fair to the other employees." Ms. Peters looked at Shasta for a response.

Shasta remained careful with the facial expressions she exposed. Momma told her, facial expressions are deadly. She didn't want to give Ms. Peters the pleasure to say anything smart to her. "Very well Ms. Peters, I'll see you in forty minutes."

Ms. Peters smirked at Shasta and walked back to the floor. Shasta rolled her eyes after Ms. Peters left. She despised Ms. Peters, yet she had to work with her. She didn't care for the job or the paycheck, but she had to make a living somehow. Shasta's dream career was working in a restaurant. Maybe being a manager there. She started saving a few months ago. Laquenta decided to jump on the band wagon too. With the restaurant job in mind, Shasta knew she was going to have to hold the smart remarks when it came to Ms. Peters. Shasta had a dream to fulfill and she wasn't going to allow someone as ignorant as Ms. Peters stop her.

After waiting the short forty minutes, Shasta clocked in on time as promised. She went to the register and waited for the customers. She knew the day was going to be slow. It was a hot Wednesday afternoon, customers were either at work, or enjoying their day off somewhere else besides the discount store.

Shasta cleaned up her area and watched as Emily straightened clothes up on the racks. Shasta giggled as Emily made faces behind Ms. Peters back. She and Emily had built a great bond at work. Besides Laquenta, Emily was the only other female she trusted.

By four Shasta was desperate for a break. She knew she had to work at least four hours to get a fifteen minute break but she wanted a cold soda. Ms. Peters was in the back doing inventory. She was thankful she wasn't up front with her eagle eyes, watching her every move. She got a can soda from the small refrigerator at the front of the store and deposited 25 cents into her cashier drawer. She took several quick swallows of the ice cold liquid. She instantly became refreshed. A heat wave started at eleven and it seemed it had no plans of cooling down in the foreseeable future.

Emily talked to a customer near the middle of the store and above her was a huge ceiling fan circulating cool air, for the moment. Shasta needed to cool down. She had manned the front counter for the past three and a half hours and needed to breathe. Nobody was at the checkout counter. She walked over to Emily and the customer. Their conversation had ended; she and Emily talked easily about nothing in particular. Two young women walked in the store to look around. The young Mexican girl walked past Shasta and Emily and went down the shoe isle. The other girl, a tall black girl stayed near the front looking at a magazine. Ms. Peters was coming from the back and told Emily she wanted her to bring some of the tagged items to the front. Shasta was walking up to the front and was nearly knocked over, as the Mexican girl raced past her. She said, 'Go' to the tall girl and they ran from the store as the devil himself was running behind them. Shasta looked around in confusion but realization registered on her face as she realized what happened.

Ms. Peters walked swiftly over to where Shasta stood with her mouth agape and let out a huge bellow. "Why didn't you stop them? Why didn't you! I'll tell you why you didn't stop them, it's because you're in on it with them. Those girls just stole from this store and you did nothing to stop them. Wait until Mr. Gillian learns of your betrayal." Ms. Peters stormed off to the back and Shasta stared after her in stunned silence. Ms. Peters was wrong for yelling at her that way, yet telling Mr. Gillian was not good in Shasta's eyes. He'd flip out once he heard what happened.

"Don't worry about her. Mr. Gillian won't believe you had anything to do with those girls stealing. It's crazy that she'd even accuse you of something..."

"That's just it, it's not crazy to me. It's never been a secret of her dislike for me. I wonder how far she'd go with this..."

"She can't prove anything. It'll be okay." Emily walked off toward the bathroom but Shasta wasn't confident. She had a weird feeling Ms. Peters was far from through with her.

******

Shasta didn't bother to tell momma what happened at work. It would only make momma get upset. If anything drastic happened, Shasta wouldn't have a choice but to tell momma.

It was 6:55pm, five minutes until her conversation with Seth. That's what kept her smiling all day. She can't wait to hear his smooth, deep voice. Momma went to bed early; she had a long day ahead of her tomorrow. Cassie left with her husband, and Shasta was in the kitchen washing dishes waiting by the phone.

A minute to seven o'clock.... her heart raced as she thought of what to talk about. *What if I can't hold a conversation? What if he isn't attracted to me? What if he doesn't call?* All these thoughts were frustrating her. She rinsed off a plate when the phone rang. She rushed toward the wall to pick it up before it rang again. "Hello," Shasta said in her sweet voice. She walked back to the kitchen sink and continued to wash the dishes. She was glad the cord reached to the kitchen sink.

"Hello Shasta, how are you?" Seth asked.

"I'm okay, better now that you called."

"I told you I was going to call...and I am a man of my word. How was your day today?" He asked.

Shasta sighed, she was reluctant to tell Seth what happened at work today, but it was bothering her. She needed to talk to someone about it before she exploded. "Work was horrible my supervisor accused me of something I didn't do."

"What happened?" he asked sounding seriously concerned.

"I didn't plan on talking to you about this." She said as she walked to the kitchen table. Silverware was in the sink but Shasta knew she'd tend to that later. She rubbed her hands through her hair as she replayed what happened in her mind.

"Don't worry about it, I hate when you're upset or feel down, it makes me upset. So...what happened?"

"Two girls came into the store today and stole a few things; I was stunned when it happened. Both girls were minorities and my supervisor believes I had something to do with it."

"Really?"

"I'm not Ms. Peter's favorite if you know what I mean. When she first saw me working at the register, she had complaints. A few weeks ago she was mad I didn't have customers in my line. It wasn't my fault, the store was practically dead!"

"Wow, I'm sorry you had to go through that today." Seth said sincerely.

"It's okay, I haven't told anyone else what happen besides Emily. She witnessed the entire thing, she's the co-worker that I pick up and take home sometimes."

"I'm glad you got that off your chest. Well, my day wasn't too bad. I washed cars all day, but at least it felt good outside."

"I agree we did have some beautiful weather today." Shasta said. It remained quiet for a few minutes. Shasta was still nervous playing with the phone cord. She continued to smile from ear to ear as she listened to Seth breathe.

"Well...uh...I want to really go out with you this weekend. I want to take you to the picture show. You talk to Laquenta about it yet?"

"Oh yeah, I sure did. We'll meet at eight." She replied.

"That's fine with me. Shasta..."

"Yes?" she responded.

"I'm really attracted to you. I don't mean to be forward but I want to date you on a serious level. I know we just met but I don't want this to end and I don't want anyone else to get the chance to sweep you off your feet."

Shasta was glad Seth couldn't see her blushing, "I don't think you have to worryabout that. We could start dating seriously but we have to go out to the picture show first. I don't know if I want to tolerate you." She giggled.

Seth laughed. It was good to hear some laughter today. Shasta's night turned a corner. She knew talking to Seth was going to make her feel good, but not this good. She was excited for the show this weekend which was a couple of days away. She couldn't wait to see how things were going to turn out between them. She was closer to experiencing the meaning of true love. She was glad it was with Seth who would possibly be the guy to show her.

Chapter 5

The big day was finally here. Shasta was excited. Ms. Peters hadn't been in the last few days and Shasta was happy beyond words. She heard she was sick and this was music to Shasta's ears. Nobody heard from Mr. Gillian and Shasta wondered if Ms. Peters called him about the incident. Momma went to a church function with a friend and Shasta had the house to herself to prepare for her date.

Laquenta was going to pick her up for the picture show, but that was hours from now. Shasta wanted to look pretty. She searched through the closet to see what she could wear. She pulled her neck length hair up and pinned it. She didn't like the look, so she dug out the curling iron from the bottom drawer in the bathroom. She got out of the shower a few minutes earlier and stood in the bathroom with her pink and white cotton robe. She painted her toe nails the night before and applied a clear nail harder to her fingernails. A pink and purple belt-less dress hung on a hanger in her bedroom for her to wear this evening. Although everything was set, she still was nervous.

As her stomach did somersaults, Shasta thought of the evening ahead. Seth was taking her to see *Lady Sings the Blues* and she had a couple of hours to spend with Seth afterwards. She wished it was longer but Momma was coming straight home after church and Laquenta had an early morning engagement she had to attend. She had three hours to spend with Seth. She smiled despite the butterflies threatening to free themselves from her belly. She needed to figure out her footwear still. She couldn't decide on flats or sandals. She looked at the clock with angst. *Where had the time gone?* Laquenta was arriving within the hour. Her indecision unnerved her some times. She only had a few selections of sandals as it was. The time deciding on the flats or three pair of sandals caught up with her. Her hair looked okay but once she put on the dress, it would look untamed. She ran into the bedroom and grabbed the dress off the hanger.

When she made back into the bathroom, a tear ripped in her stockings. Now what? Her nerves were getting the best of her. She quickly stripped of the stockings and decided to go without them. She lifted the dress over her head and smoothed it out. She admired herself in the mirror and tested the curling iron. It was perfect. She proceeded to put several fat curls to the sides and back of her hair. Satisfied with the look, she ran into her mother's room and grabbed the pearl drop earrings in the clear jewelry box sitting on the dresser.

Momma and Shasta weren't really into necklaces but really adored earrings. Going into her bedroom, she looked down at the shoes near the foot of the bed. She closed her eyes and did an eny meny miny moe. Her finger settled on the black criss cross sandals and she quickly put them on.

Shasta waited on the sofa for Laquenta to pull up. She sat and twiddled with her fingers, curious on what lay ahead of her. She wondered if he really wanted to be with her and where they would be a year from now. She didn't imagine having a serious relationship with a white boy, but you can't help who you fall in love with, despite their race.

The loud honking noise startled Shasta because she'd fallen deep in thought. She looked out the window and Laquenta was waving for her to come outside. She grabbed her purse off the coffee table, her keys and locked the door. The closer she walked to the car, the closer she was to seeing Seth.

"Don't you look all dolled up," Laquenta smirked as Shasta got in the car.

Laquenta looked into the mirror on the side of the car to make sure her lipstick was in place, before pulling off. "So you ready to go?" She asked noticing how nervous Shasta looked. She swallowed hard before answering, "Y...yes...I'm ready."

"Girl they're just boys, don't be nervous. Seth is a great guy. It's not a blind date or anything." Laquenta's words were a bit soothing to her, yet she was still nervous. Shasta longed to know what was going on in Seth's mind at that moment. She just wanted the date to go well.

****

Shasta's heart pounded a thousand miles a minute when Seth sat next to her. Neil thought it would be a great idea for them to meet inside the theater instead of outside. Seth's warm smell saturated Shasta, the selection of his cologne was perfect, no matter how many times she smelled it. She adored it.

Seth smiled, gazing at her as the previews played. Seth and Shasta sat at the top of the theater. Shasta knew he was looking at her but she didn't dare look back, unaware of how to respond or what to do. Neil and Laquenta sat on the other side of the same row. Not too many people were out to see the show. The older couples sat closer to the front. Seth picked a great day.

"It's great to see you again." Seth said as he rubbed his hand against hers.

"Yes...it's always great to see you. How was your day?" She asked.

"It's better now that I am sitting next to you." He winked. He placed his hand on Shasta's leg. She was a bit hesitant to touch him but she couldn't resist the smile on his face. Their hands intertwined and Shasta's world stopped. Seth was making himself aware of his surroundings before he made any sudden moves. When the coast was clear he placed his lips on her cheek. He kept his eyes open making sure no one was looking at them.

"I don't want this night to end." Shasta whispered into Seth's ear.

"Don't worry, we'll have plenty of moments to share together. Just enjoy the now and we will focus on the future later."

Seth kept his head low throughout the movie. He wore a ball cap intentionally so people wouldn't see him with Shasta. Thankfully it was dark, but he knew if he wanted to continue to see Shasta again, this was the way it was going to be.

Shasta rested her head on his shoulder. The returning smell of his cologne made her reminisce about the day they first met, although it was a few weeks ago, she knew she wasn't going to ever forget that day. That day was the best day of her life, and she knew she had more to come.

****

The night was coming to an end and Shasta dreaded it. Her Ma would be home in twenty minutes and she wanted to beat her there, take off her clothes and put on a night gown. She smiled as she thought back on the evening. She had felt secure with Seth. She had a few moments of nervous butterflies when she realized her sister's cousin by marriage was three rows ahead of her and just to the right of Seth. She'd been ill at ease. The hairs on her arms rose and were akin to static on the TV. Seth had turned to her and squeezed her hand. That was reassuring but not a moment later, she felt a hate so strong that it had her looking around the theater in angst.

While Tabitha would find her choice of men distasteful and make trouble for her with Cassie, she knew she didn't hate her. The strong dislike was coming from somewhere else but where? She closed her eyes and chose not to give into the inner turbulence she was feeling, if just this once. Tonight was a special night and Seth was her man. Her man. She was finally happy and she owed that all to Seth.

Chapter 6

Shasta had one more hour ahead of her. She was there for eight hours, however thinking about Seth made it go by fast. She didn't really remember what the movie was about. All she could think about was Seth's cologne and his smile. He had a million dollar smile and could possibly get away with anything.

"Why you so quiet today?" Emily asked. She was standing next to her with her arms crossed. "All you've been doing was smiling, what's up with you?" She said. Sometimes Shasta would forget that Emily was white, the more Emily hung around her, the more urban she sounded.

"Me...I'm not quiet, nowhere near quiet. I've just been thinking." Shasta looked around to see if Ms. Peters was around, she knew she couldn't afford to get in anymore trouble.

"I see...so how was the date?" Emily asked again. Shasta walked around her counter to stand closer to Emily. "It was wonderful. Seth is amazing and I know for certain he is the one!" She said grinning from ear to ear. She looked like a little girl in a candy store, or a kid who was going to Disney World for the first time.

"That's nice." Emily scoffed.

"What's wrong with you, aren't you happy for me?" Shasta asked sounding confused.

"Of course I'm happy for you. I'm glad to see there is someone for you, I just..."

"You just what," Shasta replied loudly.

"I want a boyfriend...I want to know what it's like to be in love."

"No worries, you will get one. You just can't have mine. Just joking but I thought I would never get a boyfriend but now...I know love is possible for me. Just hang in there."

"Yeah. You're right, I'll hang in there." Emily said as a lady approached the counter with a few items. Emily went to ring the lady up while Shasta closed out her cash register.

"Are you going to be okay going home tonight or are you going to need a ride?" Shasta asked as she walked toward the door.

"I should be fine, I asked my mom if she can come and get me, she said she will."

"Okay,well see you tomorrow. Remember love is just around the corner." Shasta said. She felt as if she was giving Emily great advice.

Shasta drove home with Seth still on her mind. She was thinking about calling him tonight and scheduling to meet up with him later this week. She knew going days without seeing him would be hard for her.

The moment Shasta pulled up to her house she noticed her sister sitting on the porch. Momma wasn't home yet and she couldn't understand what her sister wanted. It was rare that they talked, maybe she was waiting for momma to come home.

"Hey, how was work?" Cassie asked.

"It was cool. You waiting for momma? What happen to your key?I thought she gave you a spare one." Shasta asked as she approached her sister.

"I specifically came here to talk to you. Tabitha told me she saw you the other day at the picture show. Who was the guy that you were with? Momma told me you went to the picture show with Laquenta." Cassie stated, she didn't look too pleased about the conversation.

"He's just a friend." Shasta said looking at the front door. She wished she could walk through it and not have this conversation with her sister.

"Just a friend, you don't have to lie to me Shasta. I'm not momma. So what's he like?" She asked smiling.

Shasta sighed in relief, she was glad to know Cassie approved of her talking to Seth. "He's so handsome and I know for a fact you'll like him. He treated me like lady and he's so cute. I met him at a picnic with Laquenta last month."

"Oh the food you was slaving over...that was for the picnic? Too bad I never made it out there." Cassie laughed. "I should've known you were up to something."

Shasta grinned.

"So he's white right." Cassie confirmed. She knew she couldn't have this conversation with momma around. She would have a fit knowing Shasta was dating outside her race.

"Yes he is," Shasta said proudly, "love doesn't have a color."

"Right, well I'm only telling you this because I love you. Don't think something strong is going to come out of this relationship. Now I'm going to let you have your little fun and I won't say anything to momma but if this relationship gets too serious ,I think you need to think twice about where you're going with Seth." Cassie said, she stood up and followed Shasta into the house.

Shasta wasn't in the mood to hear that, "This world is so limited. Why does it matter who I date?I like Seth and he likes me. I'm not hurting anyone by dating him."

"I didn't say you were hurting anyone but knowing how society is...interracial relationships are not allowed. It's just the way it is."

"Whatever," Shasta scoffed. She couldn't believe her sister was saying this to her. " I like Seth and he likes me," Shasta kept stating.

"I can see that, for you to go to the picture show with him was pretty bold. The next outing you guys go to you need to make sure..."

"I don't need to make sure of anything, if I want to date Seth that is what I'm going to do. I'm going to go wherever I please and do whatever I want and if Seth and I have sex, I am going to enjoy that too!" Shasta stormed upstairs to her room and slammed the door. She flopped down on her bed and covered her head with her pillow. She knew Seth was the one for her despite what Cassie or anyone else thought.

Chapter 7

Shasta got to work early and was surprised to see Emily at her locker. Shasta spoke and Emily gave her a dry hello.

" How did you get to work? I tried to call your house twice but got no answer." Shasta asked.

" I got dropped off." Came Emily's response, leaving Shasta to wonder what was really going on. Emily had gotten dropped off before but she usually let her know she didn't need a ride ahead of time. She seemed distant today. Shasta decided to leave well enough alone.

" Okay. I'm heading up front." No sooner did the words come out of Shasta's mouth, did Emily run past her toward the front of the store. Shasta looked on with her mouth agape for a moment or two and proceeded to the front of the store as well. Ms. Peters was somewhere in the back of the store. Shasta could smell her nasty cigarette and briefly closed her eyes. She dreaded seeing Ms. Peters today more than any other day. Today was her six month evaluation and if the past few weeks were any indication, she would more than likely get a failing evaluation.

Shasta could feel a splitting headache coming on. It was early and she had a whole seven hour shift to complete but she prayed the time would go by quickly.

Her prayer was answered some what because three women entered the store not long after she counted her drawer and got several bath towels, sand buckets, flip flops and a huge water cooler. It was just the distraction she needed. Not long after the women left, the customers started coming in at a steady pace and before long, it was time for her first break.

Shasta saw that Emily was no longer talking to her customer and she was about to tell her she was going on break, when Ms. Peters walked up front. As if sensing what she was about to say to her, Ms. Peters began speaking; " There will be no fifteen minute breaks today. You each get your lunch break and no more. There's much to do. Now grab your water bottles and get back to work." Ms. Peters said sternly and walked off toward the back room. Shasta looked over at Emily but she refused to make eye contact. Shasta sighed and did take a huge swig of her water. It was a little warm but she needed it.

She had a cold one in the back but she knew Ms. Peters was watching her like a hawk so she began stocking some of the candy up by the cash register. She got a light rush of customers, then just as she was about to inform Emily that she was taking her lunch break for real this time, Seth walked in. She didn't realize it was him at first because her back was turned but his unique scent caused her to turn around. The butterflies in her stomach were only marching in a line this time and not doing sommersaults but their measured effect left her weak in the knees. Seth turned his dazzling smile on her and she was lost.

"What are you doing here?" She didn't want to sound unthankful. She was thrilled to see him but could she slip away before Ms. Peters saw them together? She grinned secretly. How would Ms. Peters know he wasn't just another paying customer? This could be fun after all. Since Emily only had to run the register when she was on break or helping a customer, Seth would be the customer that she needed to assist today. Ms. Peters couldn't be mad if she helped out a customer, right?

"I kinda thought you would be glad to see me. You are aren't you?"

" Of course. You need help locating the picnic supplies right? I can help you." Shasta said and when Seth smiled, her whole heart melted.

" Yes ma'am. I need assistance with the picnic supplies and you seem to be just the one to help me. You lead the way." Seth said and Shasta led him toward the picnic isle. Shasta was so excited. She no longer wanted Emily to run the counter. She would be the one to ring Seth up, and at the same time, she would spend every second she could with him.

******

Shasta led Seth down the picnic isle and picked up a blue, checkered picnic throw and handed it to Seth. She then picked out a small basket and handed it to him. She saw Ms. Peters walk out of the office but she turned around when she heard the phone ring. Shasta walked over toward checkout with Seth close behind her. She didn't notice Emily watching them from her position in the clothing isle.

“Is this a hint or something?” Seth asked lighting up the room with his mega watt smile. Shasta blushed but the sound of Ms. Peters getting off the phone made her remember where she was and she began ringing up Seth's purchases.

“I'll give you my discount, ok. It's only 10% but it's better than nothing.”

“I'll take whatever you have to give me.” Shasta said nothing but she wrung up Seth's purchases. It was going on 1:00 p.m and she was going on her break this time. If Emily wanted to take hers, it would be when she returned from her break. She was taking every last minute too.

“That's $5.36 please.”

“That's pretty cheap. Are you sure that's all it is?” Seth asked, shaking his head.

" Yep, that's it. I'm going to take my break now." Shasta whispered and Seth nodded. Shasta went over to tell Emily that she was talking her break now and would be back at 1:35. Emily nodded but continued to look toward the register. Ms. Peters was walking toward the front just as Shasta walked out the front door.

Outside, Shasta let out a sigh of relief. Seth had parked around the corner, toward the side of the building and was already in his car. As soon as he saw Shasta approach, he walked over and opened the door for her.

"I didn't know you were coming straight out. I thought you had to clock out or something."

"We don't have to so I just came out. My purse is back there but I have no cash in it so I'm fine." Shasta replied and rubbed her icy hands. Seth put the car in reverse and drove down the street a ways toward a nearby burger joint. Shasta was thankful because she was hungry but more thirsty than anything.

Seth ordered them both burgers and cokes. He parked around the back, off to the side and they enjoyed their meal and made light conversation. Seth held her ice cold hands and like magic, they began to get warm. He kissed her knuckles and Shasta was ready for his lips on something else when she caught a glimpse of his watch. It was 1:29 and time to get back to the discount store. The time had flew and she didn't want to go back but knew she had to. She touched Seth's wrist and he nodded and drove back toward the store.

Shasta got back to the store just in time before Ms. Peters would consider her late. She knew Ms. Peters would be waiting to right her up for anything. Shasta stood at the register looking around the store trying to hide her smile. She felt bubbly inside and couldn't wait to see Seth again. While ringing up a customer she reminisced Seth kissing her on the cheek before she rushed back into work. She had a full stomach and a smile to match.

"You seem to be in a good mood." the customer stated after Shasta gave her the total.

"I am," Shasta replied, "it's a good day today,"

"I guess." she replied. "As hot as it is outside it can make anyone have a bad attitude. My house is so hot my candles are melting, that's why I had to run here and buy not one but two fans." She said holding up her two fingers.

"Well those are the best fans we have in the store, I believe you will be satisfied once you get home."

"I hope so, because if I'm not, I'm coming back here and returning them." She said as she wobbled her way out the door. Shasta watched as she slowly moved left to right, making her way out.

Chapter 8

Shasta had to talk to Laquenta. She drove past her house to see if she was home. She usually was because Laquenta rarely went out anywhere after work.

"Hello Mrs. Holmes. Is Laquenta home?" Shasta asked after Mrs. Holmes answered the door. She was covered in flour and it was obvious Mrs. Holmes was attempting to make dinner. Laquenta always complained about her momma's cooking, that's why she tried so hard to learn how to cook. Mrs. Holmes looked flustered answering the door.

"Yes baby, she's upstairs, just go on up there. She ain't doing nothing." Mrs. Holmes replied.

Shasta did just as she was told. She knocked on the door and Laquenta shouted for her to come in. She opened the door to find her friend fixing her hair.

"Where you going?" Shasta asked standing in the doorway.

"Nowhere, I just want to press my hair so that it's all nice and pretty. I hate when it's fizzy." She made a face after she parted a piece of her hair with her fingers. "What brings you over here? I haven't seen you in about a week."

"I've been at home...talking to Seth. He came past the job today." Shasta said smiling,

"Oh really." Laquenta put down the curlers and pulled Shasta in from the doorway. "Have a seat. You have to let me know what happened. Did he know you worked there?What made him come in there?"

"I don't know. I mean, he knows I work at a discount store but I don't know what made him come in. He got a few things and just as he was leaving it was time for my break, so we went to the burger joint up the street and made small talk. He kissed me on the cheek...right here." She said pointing to the left side of her face.

"Aww, how cute. You and your boo having lunch." Laquenta teased. "So what else happened?"

"Nothing really," Shasta said looking around the room, "but Emily had an attitude with me all day and she said something that really bothered me."

"What'd she say?" Laquenta asked.

"She told me Seth shouldn't be dating me because I'm not white." Shasta said ,her face downcast.

"Let me tell you something." Laquenta said making sure her door was locked. What Shasta just told her made her furious. She knew how sensitive Shasta was and how she wanted everyone to be her friend. "No one is going to like you dating Seth. I have issues with it myself. You should see the looks on people's face when I am in public with my guy. But guess what..."

"What," Shasta said.

"I don't give a rats ass what they think. I went out to the restaurant the other day and they wouldn't serve us because I was with him. I was mad but that didn't affect our relationship. If Seth really wants to be with you...and if you re*ally* want to be with him, you gotta do whatever it takes to stay strong. You're not going to have a lot of support, hell...I may be your only support but if you let Emily's words hurt you, then you're in for a rude awakening."

"I just don't understand. What's the big deal in me dating Seth, as long as I am happy that's all that should matter." Shasta replied.

"You're right, maybe in twenty years it will be like that or maybe it will never be like that. Society doesn't look kindly to black and whites having relationships like that with each other."

"I don't know...I mean I really like Seth but..."

"But what...you gonna let some little white girl stop you from dating Seth? You like him right?"

"Yes." Shasta said in almost a whisper.

"You want him to be your first love?" Laquenta asked with her hands on her hip.

"I...I do, I want to know what love is. I like being around him and the way he makes me feel..."

"Exactly, don't let these fools stop you from being happy." Laquenta said, sounding like her mother. Shasta didn't know what to expect but she knew she wasn't going to let Seth go that easy.

****

Shasta's walked into momma's room to make sure she was sleep. She kissed her on the forehead and tiptoed downstairs. She had to talk to Seth, she couldn't grasp Emily having an attitude toward her. *How am I supposed to face society if I can't even face a co-worker?* She knew talking to Seth would make her feel better. Laquenta made some good points but she wanted to hear those points from Seth too.

"Hello, can you talk?" Shasta asked immediately as Seth picked up the phone. She hated sounding like a white girl when someone else answered the phone. She was relieved when she heard his voice.

"Yes, you couldn't have called at a better time. My father gave me my own phone line. The car wash business is doing so well he wanted to have the old line available for business purposes."

"Oh how nice. So how was the rest of your day?" She asked making small talk.

"It was good. I went back to the shop and washed about ten cars. My father had me working so hard but I made some good money. I couldn't help but think about you all day. I want to see you again. What are you doing tomorrow?" He asked eagerly.

"I have to go to work, then I have to help momma around the house She wants to cook and Lord knows I can use more time with momma in the kitchen."

Seth chuckled. "Okay well when are you available?"

"Uh...I don't know. I have to get back to you on that one. But look Seth, when I came back from work, my co-worker was upset with me."

"Why...what happened?" His voice was deep yet he sounded so concerned. He made Shasta feel protected even when he wasn't around her.

"She was upset because you and I are dating. She said..." Shasta sighed. "She said that white guys and black girls shouldn't be dating. She's upset because we spent lunch together. I don't know what to do. I didn't think people cared so much about interracial couples." She stated. She let out another loud sigh wondering what Seth's response was going to be.

"You know something...that's going to happen. I don't know what to expect from other people but I do know one thing."

"What's that?"

"I care about you. I like being around you and I want to continue to have a relationship with you. I want you to be my girlfriend and if that means I have to cut ties with all my friends and family, then so be it. It's not going to be easy but the feeling I have when I am with you…it's indescribable. I've never felt this way about anyone else and I don't think I ever will."

"That means a lot to me. I'm glad we are on the same page. I was talking to Laquenta and she was saying the same thing." Shasta's heart melted like a popsicle on a hot summer day. "I just don't want to be alone."

"Sweetheart you're not alone and as long as you are with me, you never will be." Seth said with such confidence. She continued to listen to Seth as he talked about where he saw them in the future. She hugged on to the phone so tight smiling from ear to ear.

Chapter 9

Shasta got off the phone and was doing a twirl, just as momma came into the kitchen. Momma looked at her strangely and poured herself a glass of iced tea before sitting down at the dining room table.

"Girl what's wrong with you? You not on that crazy stuff that girl down the street is on are you? I have no place for that mess in my house, you hear me? I didn't raise you to be no druggie. You better drop to your knees and pray to the Lord for deliverance. He'll work wonders on your spirit."

"Momma, it's nothing like that. I was just happy was all."

"Happy about what? You work at a job that your direct boss is clearly a racist and can't stand you. Honestly, I'm surprised you still have a job there. I would not be working in such a hostile environment."

"Momma, it's not as bad as all that. Really it isn't..."

"Now Debra Holmes told me that Ms. Peters is a trifling, hag of a woman. If you want me to go up there and put my two cents in, she'll not only be kissing your butt but she'll be kissing everything in between too." Shasta shook her head but knew her momma was serious. Her momma was a thick, healthy, cornbread and cabbage eating woman born in the deep south. Ms.

Peters was rail thin and rivaled Olive Oil in looks and statue. Ms. Peters wanted no parts of momma on any given day. Even when momma was sick, momma could take her hands down.

"Momma, it's okay. Really it is. I don't even pay attention to that woman. I just do my job and that's it."

"Just watch her. She isn't to be trusted." Shasta had to agree. Ms. Peters wasn't to be trusted but now neither was Emily. She had to wonder how far Emily would go to prove to her that she and Seth didn't belong together. Unfortunately for her, she would find out sooner, than later.

****

Shasta got to work a few minutes before she had to clock in. Emily wasn't there yet and Shasta was secretly thankful. Ms. Peters raggedy old Buick was parked in its normal parking space but she had yet to see her. She clocked in and put on her apron. She was heading to the front when she heard footsteps from behind her and turned to see Emily coming out of the back room. Shasta looked stunned but said nothing. Emily proceeded to walk past her as if she wasn't even there.

Shasta ignored her too but not because she really wanted to. A customer had come in with a big dog and the dog was running around the store. The owner ran after the dog but the dog was fast for its enormous size. The owner finally got the dog under control just as

Shasta was coming to assist the lady. The lady made the dog sit by the door as she gathered her things to purchase. Shasta watched the lady and the dog, who sat quietly by the front door. Suddenly, the door chimed and Emily walked inside.

Shasta looked confused and was about to say something when the lady came back with her items to be wrung up. Shasta wrung her out quickly and looked for Emily down one of the many aisles. She didn't see her anywhere. She was upset with Emily for snubbing her but she was a little nervous too. It was nearly 9:30 and Ms. Peters had not shown her face nor had she heard her talking or anything.

A curious moment came ten minutes later as Shasta was with a customer. Surprisingly, Emily's half sister and her Aunt Tanya came into the store. Emily's half sister headed straight toward Shasta and dropped a bottle of lighter fluid on the counter. The customer Shasta was with left after his purchase and Shasta turned her attention to Emily's half sister.

"Can I help you?" Shasta asked and chanced a look at Emily's Aunt Tanya who had her head down. Tanya would not look at Shasta for nothing in the world but Emily's sister seemed to be all piss and vinegar.

"Yeah, you can help. I want a refund for this lighter fluid. It ain't been opened." Shasta looked at the bottle and pushed it away, shaking her head.

"We don't sell that kind of lighter fluid. Maybe you got it from another store."

"Naw, naw. It's y'alls brand. Give me my 75 cents."

"We don't sell that brand here. We sell a generic brand named Flame and a more popular brand name Kingston. That had to come from another store."

"I don't think so. Emily, Emily. Come up here girl." Emily's sister yelled and again, Emily appeared from nowhere. Shasta looked on in stunned disbelief as Emily walked up to the counter with what appeared to be a bottle of lighter fluid. Just as Emily set the bottle of lighter fluid on the counter, Ms. Peters came through the front door.

"There looks to be a little commotion going on, is there something I can help you with?" Ms. Peter's asked Emily's sister.

"Yes," the girl responded, "your employee here was giving me a hard time about returning my lighter fluid."

Ms. Peters darted her eyes to Shasta."Is this true?"

"I told her we didn't have this brand, I can't return something that we don't sell."

"We do sell it Ms. Peter's I just walked up and took the lighter fluid from off the shelf. Shasta's just too lazy to even look to see if we had it." Emily butted in. Shasta looked at Emily and shook her head. "We don't sale this brand!" Shasta yelled, she was becoming furious and believed this was a set up.

"Of course we do. How do you think Emily was able to put it on the counter? Give her refund and after that I want you to leave. You're suspended without pay for the next week." Ms. Peter's said. Emily and her sister were snickering as Ms. Peter's walked away.

"Excuse me?" Shasta was in awe, she couldn't believe Ms. Peter's embarrassed her like that in front of a customer.

Shasta did what she was told, clocked out and headed back home. She couldn't believe she was only at work for forty-five minutes and something like this happened. She knew from that moment on, her and Emily's friendship was over.

****

"What are you doing home so early?" Momma asked when Shasta walked through the door. She wasn't sure how she was going to tell Momma but it wouldn't be much longer before she found out.

Shasta sighed. "Nothing happened." She tried walking upstairs to her room but momma wasn't having it.

"What happen at work Shasta?" Momma followed her to her room. One thing about Momma, she never would leave you alone until her question was answered.

"I got put on suspension, that's all." Shasta turned around and looked momma in the eyes, she then walked back upstairs and went to her room.

"Suspension for what?"

"Momma, can I please just go to my room. I just want to lie down. It's been a long morning." Shasta dragged herself up the rest of the stairs and closed her door. Momma must have noticed the tired look on her face because she went back downstairs and watched television.

Shasta laid on her bed and closed her eyes. W*hy was Emily doing this?* She wondered. She closed her eyes and was hoping when she got up her things would be better.

Chapter 10

Momma had to go to work the next few days, which was good because she didn't have to hear her questioning her about the job. The last thing she wanted was for momma to show up at her job and make a fool out of herself. She knew momma could take Ms. Peters any day but she didn't want momma to get in trouble behind it.

Since she had a couple of days off Shasta figured it would be nice to pay Seth a visit. He came to her job, so she wanted to return the favor. She put on her best summer dress and made her way to her man's job. Her hands were sweaty and every five minutes she was looking in the mirror making sure her hair was still fly. She knew Seth liked what he saw, but she wanted to make sure she looked perfect.

There was barely any traffic during the midday, so Shasta made it to Seth's job in no time. She pulled up to the car wash and her eyes searched for her man. She noticed him cleaning up a customer's wheels. She got out the car and headed in his direction.

"Can I be next sir," she said in her girly voice. Seth looked up and noticed a beautiful caramel girl wanting his attention. He stood up and smiled. "What brings you here today?" He looked around to make sure his father wasn't around. He then remember his father saying he had to go across town to pick up some more supplies. It was going to be at least an hour before he returned. Shasta would be long gone before his father came back. “I had a little issue at work today, so they suspendered me for a few days.” She shrugged.

“Well that’s not good.” He stood to his feet and put his hands on his frail hips. “In that case let me wash your car up, that should make you feel better. What happened at work?” He said getting back to her being on suspension.

“Emily’s sister came in talking about some stupid lighter fluid and she told me she wanted a refund. That wouldn’t have been a problem if we carried that type of lighter fluid. I knew we didn’t but she insisted that I give her a refund. Shortly after that,Emily walked up to my register and placed the same lighter fluid on the counter. Ms. Peter’s came out and told me I was suspended for trying to start conflict with a customer. She practically embarrassed me in front of customers and that’s not right...that’s not right at all.” Shasta said shaking her head with her arms folded across her chest.

“That’s stupid and I take it Ms. Peters is racist.” Seth said. Shasta shook her head.

“Let me return this car to a customer. Stay right here, I will be right back.”

"Okay." Shasta stood under a tree to get some shade, it wasn't too bad being off. At least she didn't have to be around people who didn't like her.

Seth handed the customer his keys, "Here you go sir, enjoy the rest of your day." He said.

"You too…uh…who's that girl, is she your girlfriend or something." The customer asked. He was a friend of the family so Seth knew he had to be careful what he said. "No…I just know her from somewhere. We have a few mutual friends, that's all."

"Oh ok," the guy said sounding unconvinced. "Well you be careful. You know her kind ain't really wanted around here. Tell your friend or whatever she is to not be popping up in places like this by herself. The cops will pull her over you know."

"Yeah, I'll be sure to tell her. She just wanted her car washed that's all. It's known around town that I do a mean shine…you should know. Seth said, joking with the guy.

"That's true." He smirked. He drove off in his Pontiac. Seth figured that was a close call. He enjoyed Shasta's company but he didn't want to get in trouble behind it. He had to treat her as if she was a random customer and not his girlfriend.

"Hand me your keys, I will wash you up and be right back." Seth said to Shasta, she was admiring the clean fresh air on this side of town. Everyone's grass was cut and had nice landscaping. She handed Seth her keys, just knowing his scent would be on her seats made her smile. She gazed at a couple walking down the street. They were a young white couple. She knew her and Seth couldn't ever be caught together like that. She envied the unknown couple only because she knew her and Seth could never be seen in public. Soon Seth returned her car and was wiping down her windows and tires. This gave her a chance to talk to him.

"You have to act like a customer," he warned. "I don't want anyone thinking something is up between us."

"That's understandable." she replied. "Can you make sure you wash my wheels nice like you did the other car?" She asked loudly, so other people could hear her. She thought it was a bit corny but after saying that a lot of people stopped watching them.

Seth couldn't help but laugh, he loved how Shasta played along. "So what are you going to do for the rest of the day?" He asked in almost a whisper. He wanted customers to think they were still talking about the car.

"I'm not doing anything, probably cook dinner and watch some TV." She pointed to one of the tires acting as if he missed a spot.

"That's cool, well I'm truly happy you came down here to see me. I wish I could kiss you but..."

"I know, people are watching. You know one day...this whole interracial thing is going to be a joke."

"Yeah but right now, in this day in time, we are going to have to be careful." Seth said finishing up her car. "Now you go and have yourself a great rest of the day. Call me around 9:00pm." He stated. He opened the car door for Shasta and waved as she rode off. What Seth didn't know was that his father came back earlier than expected. He watched Seth from the back window, and the way Seth was looking at Shasta he knew his son had a thing for that black girl.

****

Shasta hummed all the way home. She was humming a christian song because that's the only station that came in crystal clear in the car. She didn't dare change it because she knew her momma would have a fit. She had changed the station a few times in the past and even though she turned it back to 1570AM, her momma could tell she had fiddled with the nobs.

She was chastised three days straight and knew it wasn't worth it to turn the station anymore. The song she hummed was an old christian spiritual professing that you'll get all that you want in due time. She already knew what she wanted and that something was Seth and luckily for her, she already had him.

Chapter 11

Shasta went by the post office early the next morning. She sighed as she thought back on her phone call with Seth from the night before. They only talked about ten minutes because his mother called to him twice while he was on the phone. Seth said she didn't want anything but after Emily had turned on her, she was suspicious of everyone's intentions but Seth's.

Seth told her he had to go but not before telling her that Neil had a baseball game Wednesday afternoon and he wanted her to come with him. Shasta knew they couldn't go together but her mother would be home by 2pm and she could go the game afterward. She told Seth she would come by around 3 and that seemed to make him very happy. He told her she brightened his day and on Wednesday he would show her how she illuminated his whole world.

Shasta was so excited and couldn't wait for Wednesday to hurry and get here. Thursday she had to return to work but she didn't know how she was going to handle working there now. Ms. Peters sure had it out for her but now so did Emily. She had gotten not only her sister invloved but her aunt too. How far would they both go? She knew Ms. Peters wanted her fired and didn't like blacks in general but Emily had always been on her side until now. The more and more she thought about it, she knew it had to be about Seth.

Emily had said it wasn't fair that she was stealing a good man like Seth away from white women. She obviously had strong feelings about them seeing each other and that wasn't going to just disappear anytime soon. Shasta briefly wondered if Emily told Ms. Peters what she knew about them. She looked at her watch. If she hurried she could catch Laquenta before she left for work.

****

" Girl, what you doing at my house this time of morning? You know I gotta be to work in twenty minutes."

" I know. You just work down the street so I figured we could talk for a minute. Momma will have the car the rest of the day and when I called last night, Ms. Holmes said you were out. I.. I just..."

" Let's go out on the porch. Momma and Daddy are in the living room talking so we can talk freely out there long as we keep our voices low." Laquenta said and they sat down on the porch steps.

Usually Shasta needed a little urging but not this time. She took a deep breathe and went into her spiel. " You remember when I told you that Emily has been acting shady to me at work, well she all but called me a liar in front of Ms. Peters."

" Tell me exactly what happened." Laquenta replied and Shasta spent the next five minutes telling her friend how Emily back stabbed her, how she got suspended and how Emily got her aunt and sister in on her plot.

" Wow, that heifa is real bad news. Somebody needs to snatch her up and put a switch to her lily white ass. Ugh! Since you like Seth, she's gonna make you pay. I wouldn't be surprised if she likes him too. Why else would she truly care who you date. I think you're right. The two of them working together will only spell your destruction, unless..." Shasta moved in closer. She could hear Mrs. Holmes coming to the door. When she opened it, the two friends had scooted a few inches away from each other.

" Laquenta, why haven't you left for work and Shasta what are you doing here this time of morning? You realize it's barely eight right?"

" Yes ma'am. I was just stopping by...."

" She was stopping by but on her way to the discount store in a little bit." Shasta's eyes widened and Laquenta hurried on. " She wants to find a new job and wondered if they were hiring at my place. She did work there before and I told her, who knows when a spot might open up there. I'll be on the look out for you, okay." Shasta nodded and stood up.

"I didn't know you were unhappy there sweetheart. I know the pay is better than at Laquenta's place. It's only two girls that work there right?" Ms. Holmes asked.

"Yes, ma'am. There's me and Emily and another girl named Carly but she only works every other weekend and we're not on the same weekend. I only met her once. She works with Emily mostly and the other manager Ms. Walton."

"Well, if you feel you need to leave there, I hope you find a new job soon."

"Thanks Mrs. Holmes. I better go so you can get to work, Laquenta. Let me know what 'unless' means." Shasta whispered as she stepped off the porch. Laquenta put up the call sign with her hand and Shasta nodded. She hoped Laquenta could help her, because Lord knows she couldn't help herself.

****

Shasta didn't have to wait long. Laquenta called her around 10:30 on her first break. Her mom was out so she knew they could talk without interruptions.

"I thought about what you said honey chile and I believe it will only get worse at that job before it gets better for you, but don't let them have all the control. When you go in on Thursday, act like nothing out of the ordinary has happened. Don't talk to Emily or even make eye contact, completely ignore her. She'll secretly wonder why you haven't confronted her even if she doesn't ask you outright. Let the heifa wonder. Let her take her break before you and for how long she wants. When she gets back, tell her you are taking a break and immediately leave but make sure you do it in front of a customer."

"Why does that matter though?"

"I'm getting there. You want to make sure you tell her in front of someone in case she pretends you left without telling her. Don't leave the premises though. Go around the corner and move your car and walk back. I bet she does some underhanded stuff while you're gone like mess with your register or something."

"But if she does that, I'll be fired for sure. Ms. Peters will never take my word over hers even if I paid her to."

"Honey chile, listen and listen good. You want Emily to do something to the drawer and blame you for it. Thing is, you're going to do something to that drawer first."

Shasta had no idea what Laquenta meant but she was intrigued. Laquenta had to go back to work but Shasta wondered all afternoon about what she could mean and if she could really stick it to Emily like Emily stuck it to her. She felt Laquenta was right about one thing though, she really did think Emily liked Seth. Why wouldn't she though. He was tall, handsome and had his own money. The family business would one day be his and he had a great personality. She was envious and jealous but Shasta wanted Seth for herself and she wouldn't let Emily, Ms. Peters or anyone else take him away from her.

****

Wednesday got there before she knew it and before long, 2:00 had come and gone. Momma was on the phone with one of the mothers from the church talking about church revival and Shasta took the keys off the counter and told her mom she was going to the park for a while. She *was* going to the park but she was going to the ball park to see her man.

She got to the park just before three and noticed it was packed. She parked a block away and made her way toward the bleachers. In passing, she got a few nasty looks from the women and a few lingering looks from the men until they heard a throat clearing or a flat out '*stop* looking at her'. She knew she was in a hostile environment so she as soon as she saw Neil up at bat, she went and sat at the top seat to the far right of the bleachers. She didn't see Seth but knew he was there somewhere.

As if sensing her, Seth came into view and spotted her but he wasn't alone. There were two other white boys with him and a girl that looked to be about 8 or 9. Seth looked around briefly and realized he could do little more than just smile. He quickly flashed his pearly whites and Shasta wanted to smile back but didn't dare. Not yet anyway.

He sat half way up from where she sat. She lowered her head and did smile then. He was only four seats in front of her. She could watch him and revel in his nearness and at the same time pretend to watch the game.

Since the game had already started, Shasta wasn't surprised that twenty minutes into her watching the game, the announcer called for an intermission. Shasta moved quickly from her spot at the top because she sat near the exit. A few people were milling about but no one was really looking her way. She noticed a water fountain and was headed that way when someone tapped her on the shoulder. Her insides turned to jelly. She knew it was Seth.

"You're not leaving so soon are you?" Seth asked and Shasta shook her head.

"Not just yet but it's so packed in here. I didn't realize so many people would be here. When I paid the ticket guy the $1 he just looked at me and frowned."

"I should've told you that there would be a charge." Seth dug into his back pocket and pulled out $2.

"Here's for the ticket and why don't you put this in the gas tank." When Shasta shook her head, Seth placed the bills in her hand.

"I insist. I asked you to come and you did. I'm so happy to see you but you're right, there are a lot of people here. There's way too many eyes around." Seth looked around briefly and so did Shasta. No one was looking so Seth pulled Shasta close and kissed her on the lips. Even though his lips only lingered there for mere seconds, Shasta would never forget the feel of his lips on hers. The warm taste of mint, the softness of his lips and the blood boiling in her veins made her feel like the world was hers and everything in it.

****

"Seth, what hell are you doing with ***her?"*** A rugged white man asked as he approached the two of them. He had anger in his eyes and Shasta was scared for her life. It looked as if he was going to charge at Shasta but Seth stepped in front of her.

"This is my girlfriend," Seth said as boldly as he could. "Dad this is Shasta...Shasta this is..."

"I don't give a damn *who* she is!" He shouted, causing everyone to turn and look at him." Shasta was embarrassed because all eyes were on them.

"Well I do!" Seth shouted.

"Get your ass over here now!" He grabbed Seth leaving Shasta looking lost and confused. "I don't want you ever seeing my son again!" He yelled at Shasta, his face was dark red and spit was flying out of his mouth. Shasta covered her mouth and walked away.

"You shouldn't be here anyway, coloreds aren't allowed around here. Get outta here, get!" A spectator said. Shasta quickly walked to her car wiping the tears from her eyes. A few white children were throwing rocks at her car. She quickly drove off before any of the rocks cracked the windshield. She pulled over up the street from her house and cried, she cried for a long time. She knew if momma caught her crying she was going to have to tell the truth, and from the way Seth's father reacted she wasn't sure how momma was going to react when she found out she was kissing a white boy.

Chapter 12

Shasta rushed to her room and tried her best to avoid momma. Luckily momma was in her room laying down taking a nap. Usually she would go into momma's room and let her know she was back, but not today, not at this moment. She was too upset and heartbroken. *What did Seth's father say to him? Would she see him again? Was this the end of their relationship?* She was so confused. She didn't think someone that she liked so much would be so hard to be with. She buried her head into her pillows, wishing the pain would go away. She didn't know when the next time she would hear from Seth, which was the worst feeling of all.

Shasta didn't feel like talking to anyone. She wished she could stop breathing due to the pain and embarrassment she was feeling. She replayed the look on everyone's face when Seth's dad yelled at her. Her thoughts were interrupted when she heard a knock at the door. "Come in." She said and she turned her head toward the wall so she whoever was at the door wouldn't see her face.

"Hey sis, how's it going?"

"It's going." She mumbled.

"Momma made dinner and she wanted me to tell you that it's ready? Are you coming down to eat?" She asked.

"No...I'm really not in the mood to eat at this moment, tell momma I'm not feeling well."

"What's the matter Shasta, bad day today?" Her sister asked.

Shasta was reluctant to get up and have her sister see the tears streaming down her cheeks, but she had to talk to someone. Shasta wiped her eyes and then sat up and turned to her sister.

"What happened?" Her sister asked. She pulled the chair next to Shasta's bed.

Shasta swallowed hard and put her head between her knees. "Seth's dad caught us kissing, he embarrassed us by yelling. Everyone was starring at us and I watched Seth get pulled away by his father.

"Man...that's not good," was all her sister could say. She really wanted to say I told you so, but now was not the time to say that.

"Not at all and I don't know what's going to happen between us. I want to be with him...I really do." She lifted her head up, allowing her sister to see the tears still rolling down her face. " I think this is the end of our relationship."

"I see...that could be rough." Her sister was lost for words and Shasta knew her sister couldn't say anything that would be helpful. No one could.

"You're telling me. You're not the one dating outside your race. I just want to be happy, why does race have to hinder my happiness? I understand why whites and blacks don't get a long, but love has no color."

"It does in this day in age, Shasta. I hate to say this but if you continue to date Seth it's only going to get worse." She warned.

"I know, but I love him...I really do, I've never felt this way about anyone."

"Yeah, that's what love usually feels like." It was clear to the both of them that she wasn't the best person to talk to for advice. "I hope you feel better little sis, just hang in there. I'm going to let momma know you're not hungry or that you're exhausted or something." She got up and walked to the door. "Don't worry I'm not going to tell her about Seth."

Shasta nodded and turned her body back against the door. She felt talking to her sister was a waste of time. Who she really wanted to hear from was Seth.

Shasta paced the floor of her bedroom. It was morning now and she had barely slept a wink. Seth never called but she figured he couldn't. Still she had waited in the kitchen for endless hours with the pretense of being anxious for her first day back to work after her suspension. She really was nervous but when her mother asked her why she had fallen asleep at the kitchen table, that was the answer she gave. She didn't know what to expect with Seth and she didn't know what Laquenta had planned. That made her more nervous than anything. What did Laquenta mean by doing something to the drawer first?

Shasta opened her bedroom door and could hear momma in the kitchen humming. Shasta tip toed into the living her and went out onto the porch. Momma was too knowing and would put two and two together that her suspension was not the only thing troubling her. She had to collect her thoughts. She looked at her watch. She had just over an hour before she had to head into work. She was considering driving by Laquenta's house when she pulled up to park in front of her house. Shasta ran down the porch steps to Laquenta's car.

" I was beginning to think I dreamt the whole conversation we had the other day at your house." Shasta said and Laquenta laughed. Her laugh was cut short when she looked at her friend's face.

" I can see you didn't have a good night. Before you get into detail about what happened, let me tell you about the drawer issue. It will work if you listen to everything I tell you to do. If you go in and let either Emily or witch Peters intimidate you, the plan will go south. You'll need this." Laquenta handed Shasta a marker and motioned for her friend to come closer. Before long, Shasta was totally enthralled in her friend's plan and had renewed confidence that at least one thing this week would work in her favor.

****

Shasta walked into the discount store a minute before 9:00 a.m. Ms. Peters was up front this time and greeted her with her usual scowl that quickly became a smirk. Shasta secretly smirked too. What she had planned for those two heifas should be legendary in someone's book.

Emily was in the break room sitting but stood up the minute Shasta walked in. Shasta completely ignored her and punched in. She slipped her hand into the pocket of her jeans and sighed. She and Emily were once good friends but that all seemed like just a pretense now. Maybe Emily never truly liked her after all. She walked up to the front. She could feel Emily's eyes boring a hole in her back but she kept moving. She couldn't back down now. It was now or never.

****

" So the prodigal stool pigeon returns. What a dark cloud you bring in your wake. We had three days of sunny skies and brighteness and here you come and darken our doorstep. It feels like a thunderstorm, a tornado and a tsunami hit us all at once the moment you walked in. You're like death warmed over and reheated for tomorrow's leftovers ." Ms. Peters smirked and laughed out right and so did Emily.

Shasta didn't say a word. She went to stand by the register and Ms. Peters plopped the drawer down with force.

" The usual is in there. You count it now before I go in the back." Shasta counted the money quickly and just as Ms. Peters was about to go in the back, Shasta called her name.

" Darkie, what you want? I have things I need to do in the back and you're wasting my time." Ms. Peters said and was walking away from her.

"I need you to recount the drawer. A few of the ones are new and I wanted to make sure I had the count right."

" Damn you girl. I would've fired you months ago if I had the go ahead. It won't matter much longer anyway. We got a brand new camera installed and believe me when I say your days are numbered here." Ms. Peters replied but did count the drawer. She left hastily and Emily began stocking the shelves toward the back of the store.

There was a lot of boxes in the isles so Shasta knew Emily would be busy for a while. Shasta took out the permanent marker Laquenta gave her and began to mark the bills. The plan was simple. Shasta marked each bill with a X in the center, except the lone twenty dollar bill. For the twenty dollar bill, she put a huge circle around Jackson's face and on his forehead, she wrote the intiales 'SB' boldly and clearly. She then put the bill face down in the drawer. After she marked all the bills, she placed them back in the drawer and shut the drawer. When she got a customer who tried to hand her a twenty, she would tell them she couldn't break it until after noon but could make change for a ten or five. Most people would just try to use correct change then because no one wanted to have to wait for change to be made for them.

The plan was going smoothly. No one tried to hand her any twenties and before long it was time for her first break. She went over to tell Emily she was leaving and was surprised when Emily verbally attacked her.

" First day back and already leaving before noon. You must not want to keep your job. Maybe I should call Ms. Peters. She told me that you can't go on any breaks until after I go and I'm not going until 1:00. You'll just have to wait." Emily said snidely.

" No, I'm not. I'll be back in fifteen minutes and oh, Emily, I just counted the drawer and know there's $121 dollars in it. It better be all there when I get back." Shasta left quickly before Emily could reply and walked out the front door. She went around the side of the store where she had a perfect view of Emily and the register. The tens ,fives and ones were folded over and paper clipped. The single twenty stood alone. Emily opened the register and took out the twenty dollar bill. Shasta watched in awe as Emily pocketed the twenty and closed the register. Her plan had worked. Now all she had to was make sure Emily was caught red handed.

****

Shasta came back from her break early, just as she saw a familiar face pull out of the lot. If Laquenta's plan was to work, Mr. Gillian, the owner, should be coming any minute. Laquenta was supposed to call him from her job and pretend to be a concerned customer who frequened the store and saw one of the workers pocket some money from the register.

It was hearsay of course but Mr. Gillian didn't play around when it came to his money. Laquenta's friend Saralee was going to say she saw Emily take the money while Shasta was on break. Saralee would come back to the store when she saw Mr. Gillian pull up.

Shasta was excited and nervous all at the same time. *What if Mr. Gillian said he didn't believe Saralee? What would happen then?* Laquenta practically guaranteed he would. Saralee was a pretty red head and her family was well known to Mr. Gullian. Shasta sighed and walked through the doors. Emily smiled sardonically at her and left the counter area. Shasta smiled too. If their plan worked, it would be Emily who got sent her walking papers.

Chapter 13

Shasta watched Emily go back to her position in the isle stocking towels. Mr. Gillian opened his car door and was anxiously walking to the discount store. Shasta looked back at Emily. She had her back to her and was digging towels out of the huge box in front of her. She could hear Ms. Peters on the phone and she was secretly relived. Now if Mr. Gillian said that he was trying to reach Ms. Peters to ask her about the incident, she would be to blame for tying up the phone line.

" Where is Ms. Peters?" Mr. Gillian said as sweat beaded above his upper lip. He didn't give Shasta a chance to answer before he asked his next question.

" Are you running the register today?" He asked, still sweating and becoming red faced.

" Yes, I am sir but I just returned from my break and have not been back five minutes yet." Shasta said quietly. Mr. Gillian continued to look at her intently, then spotted Emily unloading the boxes.

" Have her get Ms. Peters. I want to get to the bottom of this right now." Shasta called to Emily and Emily ignored her. Shasta mumbled something about Emily never listening to Mr. Gillian and he then bellowed to Emily to come to the front.

Emily walked up to the front hesitantly when she saw Mr. Gillian and stood off to the side.

"This gal called you. Why didn't you come? Don't answer that, get Ms. Peters up here *NOW!"*

Emily ran to the back just as Shasta saw Saralee walk onto the sidewalk. She resisted the urge to grin and leaned back against the counter. Saralee opened the door and walked inside the discount store.

Ms. Peters made her way to the front quickly and pasted a fake smile on her face because of Mr. Gillian. Mr. Gillian didn't even wait for her to say hello. He started right in on her.

" I tried to call here several times before I drove all the way down here. The line was busy for over ten minutes, were you on the phone all that time?" Mr.Gillian asked.

" Well sir I was trying to...." Mr. Gillian hushed Ms.Peters by putting up a hand to silence her. He was sweating profusely and wiped his forehead with the back of his hand.

" I received a call barely twenty minutes ago and was told that an employee from this store took money out of the register and pocketed it. It was witnessed by a customer leaving the store. I want to know if this is true and if it is, who the **HELL** thinks they can steal money from me without me finding out and get away with it!" Mr. Gillian was beet red and Shasta noticed Emily nudge Ms.Peters and point at her. Ms.Peters nodded and walked over to where Mr. Gillian stood at the end of the counter. Neither of the three had noticed Saralee standing by a shelve of school supplies.

" Oh, I bet I can tell you exactly who's stealing money from you. The thief is right in front of you. The thief is that damn negro heathen and I suggest you fire her right this minute!" Ms. Peters replied and turned her big yellow toothed grin at Shasta. Shasta said nothing. Mr. Gillian looked at her intensely with his watery blue eyes. He opened his mouth to reply but Saralee stepped forward and touched Mr. Gillian's arm.

"Please sir. Don't do that. That young girl didn't steal a penny from your drawer but I know who did, and I have proof." All eyes turned to Saralee but Shasta was looking at Mr. Gillian. He was clearly enthralled and she could feel Laquenta's plan falling in place.

Mr. Gillian looked at Saralee and then back at Emily and Ms. Peters. Shasta stepped to the side and watched as Saralee told the truth.

"What proof do you have young lady." Mr. Gillian said in a calm tone. He folded his hands across his chest and looked at Saralee as if she was a detective solving a crime, in which she actually was.

"I noticed that young lady over there leaving for her break," she said pointing at Shasta. "Then this little one over here went into the register and took some money out. I'm the one who called HR and complained, I only came back down here because I forgot to grab another notebook."

"Is that so?" he asked.

"You can't believe her, she's just a customer, she's..." Emily shouted.

"Stop this nonsense this instant, I want you to pull out your pockets," he commanded Emily.

"B...bu...but...how you going to..."

"Empty those pockets this instant!" Shasta eyes widened as Emily put the money on the counter, it was the twenty dollar bill she circled.

"That came from my drawer." Shasta said.

"You're the one who gave this to me," Emily said yelling at Shasta, "Mr. Gillian you can't believe that customer for all we know they could be in this together."

"Did you give this to her?" Mr. Gillian asked Shasta.

"No I didn't, and if you don't believe me why don't you look on the new camera and see who really stole the money." Shasta replied.

Mr. Gillian totally forgot about installing the cameras around the store. “Hold that thought.” He relpied and went in the back with Ms. Peters and Emily to watch the recording. “Stay up front Shasta and ring this young lady out.” He said talking about Saralee. Shasta did what she was told.

“Now if there *is* evidence that you stole the money out the drawer then you might as well gather your things and never come back here again.” Mr. Gillian said as they walked to the back of the store. Emily was shaking and walking slowly, she turned back to Shasta with a sad puppy dog look on her face. Shasta shook her head and rung up Saralee’s notebook.

“Thanks girl so much for that,”

“You’re welcome,” Saralee replied. “I already owed Laquenta a favor and when she told me she needed my help I couldn’t refuse. I just hope that girl gets fired, ain’t no telling what will happen if she continues to work here any longer.” She leaned over and whispered, they both noticed a young couple walking in and they didn’t want them to hear what was going on.

“Exactly, Ms. Peters need to get fired too because she wasn’t watching over us like she's suppose to.” Shasta said. The ladies laughed and Shasta was relieved to know Emily was seconds away from getting fired.

Chapter 14

It was good to see Emily get fired. Shasta felt that Emily got what she deserved. It didn't surprise her to bare witness to Ms. Peters getting fired too. She was fired two days after Emily was. Mr. Gillian was suspicious about the time Ms. Peters would spend on the phone. He requested a bill and noticed how many hours she was in the back running her mouth on the phone. Mr. Gillian hired two new cashiers and made Shasta the manager, Mr. Gillian was a bit uncomfortable at first but Shasta was the only one who knew how to run the store. It would save Mr. Gillian time and money to train someone else to manage it full-time.

Shasta sat on her porch enjoying the afternoon sun. Laquenta pulled up in front of her house grinning from ear to ear.

"What's going on honey bun." Laquenta said as she got out the car. "Enjoying work?" Both girls laughed.

"Work is fine. Saralee told you what happened last week right?" Shasta asked.

"Yes she did!" Laquenta said slapping her hands on her knees. "I'm so glad those two muskrats are out of your life for good. So what's new?"

"Well...I did get a promotion."

"You...a promotion at the discount store, wow." Laquenta said placing her hands on her hip.

"Yeah. I didn't see it coming but Mr. Gillian said I was the only person he could trust. He didn't want to hire a new person as the manager and have to keep coming back down to the store, you know he's lazy."

"Yeah, I remember you telling me that. How often does he come to the store?"

"At least once a month and he complains about that. There are times when he don't come for two months straight." Shasta replied. "I think he got a thing for black girls." She whispered.

"He might, there's no way a white man gonna let a black girl run his store. I remember seeing him when I was at the store a few months back. I noticed how he was checking out my backside." Laquenta made a face.

"You ain't no good."

"I know. So have you heard from Seth?" She asked.

"No...not at all. It's been going on two weeks since I heard from him. I don't know what to do. It's hard erasing him from my memory. I think about him all the time. Each and every day."

"I talked to Neil and he said he hasn't heard from him either. He told me Seth told him what happened and his father watches him like a hawk." Laquenta shrugged her shoulders. "So what are you going to do?" She asked.

"I don't know, maybe I should go to the car wash."

"Go to the car wash? I'm all for backing you up but I might as well start digging your grave. If your momma found out you went to that car wash to confess your love for a white boy...girl, you know you gonna be in some mess!"

"I know. I just have to think. I know he thinks about me. What we had wasn't average, it was special...damn special. I can't just let people's opinion stop my happiness."

"That's what I say." Laquenta stomped her feet. "You just have to have a master plan."

"I know, maybe I will try to go up there when his father isn't around. He can't watch him twenty four seven."

“Yeah, that’s true but if his father’s business is as big as they say it is..”

“Who is they?” Shasta questioned.

“You know...the customers, everyone says their cash wash/detail business is bringing in a lot of money. You know people in the street talk.”

“Yeah. ” Shasta put her hands on her knees and rocked back and forth. “I need to see him. He’s like my drug.”

“Girl...I know what you mean. When I don’t see Neil for a while I get an empty feeling.”

“How are ya’ll doing anyways?” Shasta asked.

“We're doing okay but I'm tired of sneaking around. I wish I could start a petition or a rally or something. I mean...we can only go but to so many places. He plans on getting an apartment soon so spending time with him won’t be a big deal.”

“Maybe that’s what I should do.” Shasta said. “I should get an apartment so that Seth and I could be together.”

“Sounds like a plan, especially since you’ll be making more money.”

Shasta liked the sound of that. She was willing to do whatever it took to get her and Seth in the same room. She needed to tell Seth her plans, but how?

****

It had been two weeks since her promotion and two weeks since she'd heard from or seen Seth. Her mother had dropped her off at the discount store and Laquenta was going to pick her up at 7. Her days were longer now that she got promoted but she could use that extra fifty cents an hour.

She knew Ms. Peters probably made an extra seventy-five cent more an hour than what Mr. Gillian was paying her but she was just happy she still had a job, let alone a promotion that was totally unexpected.

Laquenta showed up at 7:05. She handed her a bottle of Faygo crème soda as soon as she sat down on the passenger side. Shasta twisted the lid and took a huge swig before closing the door and saying thanks.

"That's to get your adrenaline pumping." Shasta looked at her friend with askance and thought she knew what she was talking about. She was taking her to see Seth. A huge grin plastered her face as Laquenta backed out of the parking lot. The crème soda forgotten in her anticipation to see her love.

" You're taking me..."

"Apartment hunting. I got a whole list here of apartments in your price range. The first one is less than five minutes from here so if you have to walk..." Laquenta cut herself off. She silently chidded herself. She just realized Shasta thought she was taking her to see Seth.

" Sorry, honey. You thought I had news about Seth, didn't you?" Shasta nodded and Laquenta continued. " This Friday is Neil's 21st birthday. He's having a get together at Rigby Stadium on Olympius. I can't celebrate with him at the stadium but he's gonna sneak away around 9p.m. ,claiming he and some of his buddies are going for a beer run. I'm supposed to meet him three blocks from the stadium down the street on Hawley. I'm sure Seth could be one of the friends making a run with him. What do you think?"

Shasta smiled a real smile for the first time in weeks. She was sure Seth would be celebrating with Neil and although she couldn't go to the party, she would make sure she was in the car with Laquenta when she met Neil on Hawley.

" I think you're right. I think joy riding with you on Friday is just what the doctor ordered. Now about that apartment..." Laquenta showed Shasta the first apartment. The location was convient but it was a little too trashy for Shasta's taste. Several windows were boarded up and a foul odor came from up above on the second floor. The dumpster in the back was overflowing and one of the mailboxes looked like someone shot it open with a 9mm. Shasta was shaking her head and she and Laquenta hurried to the car in fear.

The apartment was only $145 a month and Shasta could see why. Who would stay there unless they had to? Sure it was in walking distance but so was one of the other apartments on Laquenta's list of four apartment complexes.

The next apartment complex was much better. You had to drive through a gate to get inside and it looked like you had to be buzzed in. Shasta eagerly got out of the car and walked up the walk leading to the apartment. Someone was coming out, so she and Laquenta walked in. The building smelled like fresh paint and had tan and red flowered paintings on the wall. Shasta really liked this apartment. She didn't know how much it cost but if it was $200 or under she was taking it.

“Did you put down a price for this complex? It's nice and clean and I would love to move in here. No foul smells from upstairs and no bullet holes in the mailbox. The mailman just puts the mail through the slit in the doors. Wow, that's amazing. You don't even have to go outside in the rain to get your mail. Imagine that!”

Shasta laughed and so did Laquenta but their laughs were cut short by a voice from above them.

"You will never move in here or any of your kind. This building is for white's only. Now get your colored asses off this property or I will call the police. By the way, you got two minutes and the clock has already started."

Laquenta and Shasta ran out the apartment complex and Laquenta had no problem speeding off. The other two complexes that were nice were in the same neighborhood.

"I don't want to be a downer but I think the other two complex tenants are going to say the same thing." Laquenta stated.

"I think so too. Did you see the look on that man's face? You would have thought we were living back in slavery times!" Shasta yelled out of frustration. "What am I suppose to do? It seems all the nice apartments are for the whites. I can't imagine what would happen if I moved into this place."

"I know. The only way you are going to move in is if you ask Seth to get an apartment." Laquenta suggested.

Shasta suddenly had a bright idea. "I can ask Seth once I see him. He's probably thinking the same thing too. I know he wants for us to be together... he probably has something up his sleeve."

"Let's put this apartment hunting on hold until we hear from Seth. It would be less stressful and from the looks of it, you could use a good shower and bed to lay in." Laquenta joked.

"Hey, I know I look a mess. Work was crazy. I don't want to ever train anyone in the near future. I had to not only do that but start inventory." she shook her head. "This is all too much."

"But it's going to be worth in when you and Seth have your own place."

"That's true. I can't say that it won't." Shasta smiled and stared out the window. She couldn't wait to see her love this upcoming week. This was going to be a long week for her.

Chapter 15

Momma was in a mood so Shasta avoided the kitchen altogether and stepped outside to get some fresh air. It was Wednesday night and she still hadn't heard from Seth but had gotten affirmation from Laquenta that he would be at the party. It was a masquerade party. Neil was turning 21 and his parents were throwing him a masquerade party. Shasta was excited. She had a long sleeve black, lace gown that her aunt had given her two years ago that she had only woren once. It was too dreadful and boring to wear anywhere but church but for an event like this, it was perfect.

The gown began high at the neck and stopped well past the knees. A pair of black stockings and a black low slung face mask should get her in the party unrecognized. That was what she sought for this event. She didn't want to be recognized by anyone but Seth. Cassie had a pair of kid boots, ankle length that she wanted to borrow. She wouldn't tell Cassie why she wanted her to loan them to her though. Lately Cassie seemed to watch her like a hawk when she came around and if truth be told, Shasta was afraid that Cassie would expose her and Seth's relationship.

She wanted to trust her sister but look what trust had gotten her so far. Emily had been a great friend but she did a 180 and nearly got her fired. As far as she was concerned, Laquenta was more trust worthy than Cassie.

She loved her sister but she couldn't truly understand her plight. Cassie was happily married with child to a black man. She didn't have to face the day to day discrimatory looks from white women who thought she was taking what belonged to them. Cassie had it easy. She just didn't get it. Laquenta did. She felt the stares, heard the whispers. She knew. She and Shasta were on equal footing.

As she sat on the porch, she reminisced about Seth's lips touching hers. His lips were so soft, like butter. She closed her eyes and hugged herself. She envisioned herself in the long, black lace gown. The hem blowing carelessly in the breeze and her sweet scent drifting over to the handsome man standing alone in the corner. As he moves closer to her, she draws in a deep breathe. She's full of anticipation as he comes out of the shadows. He moves ever closer and instantly grabs her hand and drops a kiss to her wrist. Even with the gold face mask on, she knows who it is. It's Seth....

" Girl, if you don't come get this phone! I've been calling you for the past few minutes. Quenta's on the phone. Snap out of that silly daydream and talk to this child. Make it quick. I have to call Mother Chaplin before 7:30." Her momma walked back into the house and Shasta made quick haste to the kitchen and picked up the phone. It was 7:18. She hoped Laquenta didn't want to talk long because she didn't have much time. She would call her back later but when momma was in a mood like this, she was gonna call everyone she knew and would be on the phone all night.

"Hey girl. Your momma seems like she's upset tonight."

" Yeah she is. She had a bad day at work but she's off tomorrow. She and a friend traded shifts so she works Friday instead." Shasta said and sat down at the kitchen table. She was careful to keep her voice low so momma couldn't hear her.

" That actually works out better. I told my parents I was going with friends to a jazz festival on the river. If you tell your momma that you'll meet me there around 9, she wouldn't think anything about it if she calls my mom to check in." Shasta listened and thought it sounded like the perfect plan. Her momma more than likely would call Laquenta's mom and ask about the festival and it would help if they were spinning the same story. She didn't care what they said. She would be seeing Seth in 48 hours and that was all that mattered.

******

Laquenta's planned worked like clock work. Forty-eight hours later, Shasta stood in front of her bedroom mirror looking at herself in the black lace gown. She couldn't wear it out the house because momma was laying down on the couch watching TV and was eating a late dinner. She had everything she needed for the party, even Cassie's kid boots. Shasta took the gown off and carefully placed it in a yellow satchel, along with a huge black hat and put the satchel outside her bedroom window.

She threw on a green and black sundress and pulled her hair up. The kid boots were the last to go on and she quickly tied the laces. She knew it looked strange to wear the boots with the sundress but she was afraid if she put them in the satchel, she would crush the mask or rip the gown some way.

When she came out of the bedroom, her momma was just finishing up her dinner and was watching an episode of 'Good Times'. Her mother looked up at her but didn't look at her feet. Shasta inhaled and was about to walk toward the front door when her mother called to her.

" Go put this plate and glass in the sink. You sure have been acting crazy since you got that promotion at the discount store. I think those white folks den rubbed off on you and you forgetting what color you are." Momma said and handed her the plate and glass.

Shasta knew better than to say anything so she did as she was told and stayed in the kitchen a few moments longer than necessary. She heard her momma get up from the couch during a commercial and she raced to the front door. As she was opening the door, she hollered to her mother that she was leaving and would be back later.

She didn't wait for an answer but hurried around the corner to her bedroom window and picked up the satchel. She made fast tracks to the car and pulled away from the curb. She was headed to the nearest burger joint to change clothes and then was going to see her man.

****

When Shasta got to the party, it already was pretty packed. She looked around and didn't see anyone she knew. Laquenta was there somewhere because Shasta spotted her car down the street. It was a little warm inside so Shasta walked outside to get some fresh air. She saw Neil talking to a white girl and they were laughing pretty loud. Neil put his arm around the girl's waist and whispered something in her ear. Shasta's eyes widened but a loud crash from inside the house caused her to turn around suddenly. Some fool in a white toga had spilled red punch down the front of a fairy wearing all yellow. The unassuming fairy slipped on the punch and knocked a tray of drinks to the floor.

As Shasta watched the help clean up the mess on the floor, her attention turned back to Neil. She turned around to look for him but he was no where to be seen. She closed her eyes and when she opened them, she spotted Laquenta coming from the gazebo area. She knew it was her friend because Laquenta told her that she was going to be wearing a green velvet dress and matching cape.

Shasta was about to hurry over to her friend when she smelled Seth's cologne. She knew that scent anywhere. She slowly turned around and faced him.

" Sorry to bother you but did you see a tall guy wearing a confiderate soldier outfit? It would have been tan in color and he had on black riding boots..."

" Seth, it's me. You don't recognize me?" Shasta asked. Seth looked closer at her and grabbed Shasta by the elbow and took her away from the door's entrance.

" It is you. How did you... Laquenta told you. I didn't expect to see you here tonight." Seth replied but it was what he wasn't saying that had her scared. Could it be that she was wrong? Maybe he really didn't want to be with her after all.

Chapter 16

Shasta just stared at Seth for endless moments before saying, "Maybe it wasn't such a good idea to come after all. I can see that they've gotten to you and I'm not wanted here." Shasta turned to leave but Seth wouldn't let her go. He had been holding onto her arm and had yet to release her.

"Don't say that. I didn't mean it that way at all. It's just that *my* parents told Neil's parents about us last week. His parents have been screening everyone who's here. It's obvious they didn't recognize you. Hell, I didn't recognize you either but boy you're a sight for sore eyes." Shasta grinned for the first time since she arrived. He did still want to be with her. She could hear it in his voice and more importantly, she could see it in his eyes.

They walked around a bit and talked about what his parent's reaction to the news of them dating was. Seth explained how upset his dad was and that his mom cried for three days straight. Shasta thought that was ridiculous but chose to keep quiet.

"What did your dad do to you?" Shasta asked in almost a whisper. They were alone but you could hear laughter that was getting closer. Seth took her hand and they moved further into the yard that to Shasta seemed like a huge golf course. As the moonlight shined down on them, Shasta noticed a scar above Seth's right eye. She removed her mask and gripped his chin in her hand.

"Seth what happened to you? What all did you dad say and do? When I saw you last, you didn't have that mark above your eye. What happened?"

"It's just from me being clumsy. I was washing too closely near the antenna of some guy's car. It was a dumb move..."

"Seth, this didn't come from some antenna. Did your father...did your father hit you?" Shasta finally got out and looked at Seth shaking his head in denial but the hurt was clearly chiseled in his handsome face. His dad had struck him and Shasta couldn't help but feel partially to blame.

******

Shasta caressed Seth's cheek and Seth took her hand and kissed her wrist. Seth was drawing her to him just as Shasta spotted Laquenta running toward them.

Laquenta was in a foot race and nearly ran into the both of them trying to get away. Shasta looked at Seth apologetically and took off to catch her friend.

She tracked her down not even a block away panting and out of breath. She had been crying and her mascara was running down her cheeks. Shasta approached her tentatively and placed a hand on her shoulder. Laquenta turned around and Shasta would never forget the fire and the ice she saw in her eyes. Laquenta spoke before Shasta could utter one word.

"It is officially *over* between Neil and me and I never want to date or be around another of his kind ***ever*** again! If I were you, I'd suggest you follow suit before you're left feeling like the nigger whore they all think that you are! It's all part of their twisted game. I wouldn't be surprised if Seth's in on it too." Laquenta got in her car and pulled off, leaving Shasta with more questions than answers.

******

When Shasta returned back to Seth, he stood alone under a huge oak tree. Shasta felt for Seth but knew her friend was hurting and wondered if she should leave to find her. She was about to tell Seth that she was going to try to find Laquenta and thought back to what she had seen when she came to the party. *Did Laquenta find Neil with that white girl? Was that why she said they were over? Laquenta didn't say but she had said something about a twisted game of theirs. What did Seth know and would he tell her the whole story?*

She wanted answers too. She cared deeply for Seth and didn't want to lose him but before she did something she might regret, she had to know he didn't have a part in hurting her friend.

"Seth do you know why Laquenta ran out of here the way she did? She said her and Neil are over. What happened? Please, tell me the truth." Shasta said and Seth took her hand and pulled her down beside him. They sat on the ground in front of the huge oak tree side by side. Seth took a deep breath and started spilling the beans.

"It's pretty obvious Neil parent's doesn't agree with him being in a relationship with anyone that isn't white." Seth was careful with his words because he didn't want to upset Shasta. "When Neil's parents found out about my relationship with you they had a talk with Neil, they asked if he was ever interested in color girls and he said no."

Shasta's eyes widened and she was shocked at what Seth just told her. *Did Neil really like Laquenta?* Shasta was confused but chose not to ask any questions. She continued to listen to what Seth had to say.

"He only said no because he was afraid of what would happen to Laquenta. In order to get his mother off of his back he figured the best thing to do was to act as if he had a white girlfriend, so he had one of his friends play the part. However, the girl who was "acting" as his girlfriend really liked Neil. He didn't know it but when she kissed him , I guess Neil went for it. And that's when Laquenta saw him kissing her. I wanted to run in and look for Neil because people were coming outside saying Neil just kissed a girl, and I knew they weren't talking about Laquenta because Neil isn't that stupid to kiss Laquenta at his party."

"So he really likes this girl now and whatever him and Laquenta had is over. Wow, they've been dating for almost a year."

"I know." Seth sighed. "I figured he was tired of hiding...he didn't want to continue to be in the shadows with Laquenta because it was getting to him."

"He doesn't think Laquenta had to hide too? Who in the hell do he think he is! I mean she loved the boy for God's sake." Shasta yelled as she threw her hands in the air. "So you mean to tell me when something gets too hard you guys up and quit?" Shasta got up on her feet and put her hands on her hip. She then crossed her arms because she didn't want others to recognize her attitude. It was rare that a white girl would put her hands on her hips and show attitude. Although, Seth didn't realize her reason for switching modes.

"I don't think that was his intention. It's hard for him since he lives with his parents."

"What would you do?" Shasta asked. She didn't know if this question was going to comfort or hurt her.

"I want to be with you and if that means I have to go above and beyond then that's what I would do."

"You sure as hell didn't go above and beyond after your father caught us kissing. How am I suppose to know that you're telling the truth, how can I trust you?" she asked.

Seth was silent. He didn't think explaining what happened to Neil and Laquenta would make him have to dig a deeper hole into his own grave.

"You're not going to say anything? Maybe Laquenta was right, you're just like him. I can't involve myself with someone who's weak." She stormed to her car and didn't bother to turn back. She wanted to talk to Laquenta but she knew she didn't go home and Shasta wasn't in the mood to go home either. She was upset and furious and wanted to know how her friend was doing. If she had to drive all night she was going to do just that...she needed to find Laquenta.

Chapter 17

Shasta was driving around town. She figured the best place to find Laquenta was somewhere secluded, she just didn't know where. Her mind raced with thoughts; wondering if Seth and Neil were up to some crazy ass scheme.

After driving for what seemed to be an eternity, Shasta went to the park. She noticed someone sitting by the swings. It was Laquenta and Shasta couldn't help but run to her. They hugged each other so tight that Shasta felt Laquenta's tears against her neck.

"I really loved him," Laquenta stated. "We had plans to do everything together."

"I know. I know...I talked to Seth."

Laquenta pulled back and looked hard at Shasta. "Why didn't you come after me. What made you stay and be with Seth?" She asked angrily.

"I wanted to know what was going on. I wanted to know what happened and why you were running."

"Why wouldn't you just ask me?"

Shasta didn't think Laquenta would be upset about it. She shrugged her shoulders. "I wanted to get the inside scoop. I wanted to see what Seth was going to say and he had some good information too. Don't worry I left him standing there like a bump on a log after he told me what Neil did."

"What'd he say?" Laquenta asked, wiping away her tears. They both sat on the bench as Shasta recalled what Seth had told her hours ago.

"I don't believe it one bit. I think if that was the case he would have let me in on it. Why would he ask me to come to a party and then kiss a girl?" Laquenta questioned. "If he wanted to go that route he would have chosen a girl that we both are cool with."

"True, and I felt what Seth was saying was a cover up." Shasta agreed.

******

Two days later, Shasta still had no clue what really happened or didn't happen at the party. She needed answers so she went to the car wash after she got off work. She only worked a half day and couldn't think straight while she was at work. She had talked to Laquenta on her break and had told her that she was going to talk to Seth about Neil.

Laquenta didn't say much. She was really quiet on the phone which seemed strange to Shasta and caused her to really worry about her friend. She hoped Seth had the answers she sought. Would she even know if he wore telling the truth? Things were happening so fast but she couldn't back down now. She had to just trust her instincts.

As she pulled to the back of the car wash and parked, she saw Seth talking to his little redheaded cousin. Seth took out a few dollars and gave it to the kid. The kid walked away and as soon as the kid was out of eye sight, Shasta hurried over to Seth.

"Hey. Do you want to tell me what really happened the other night?" Seth looked surprised to see Shasta standing there but took her into one of the open bays and pulled her over to the wall.

"You're right, it was more to it than what I said. Look, Neil's dad is a lot like mine in temperament. He's been known to knock Neil's mom around from time to time. Neil's dad isn't real tall but he clearly thinks he's a bigger man than what he actually is. When he's angry he yells and screams and punches things. He laid into Neil's mom the night my parents told Neil's folks about us. Neil's mom had a black eye the night of the party. It was fading but I know Neil's dad gave it to her. I guess Neil didn't want to be the cause of his mom suffering that way."

When Seth was finished, Shasta tried hard to process all he had told her. *Was Neil's dad really abusive?* He could be. Hell, Seth's dad seemed like he was abusive too. She really didn't know if the story was true or not. She just wanted to be with Seth. She wanted to feel his warm breath in her ear. She wanted to feel his arms around her. Wanted to feel his skin against hers and more than all of that, she wanted to be one with him. She just hoped he still wanted it too.

****

"You haven't said anything. You do believe me, don't you?" Seth asked and pulled her chin toward him. Shasta wanted to say yes but as unsure about Laquenta and Neil as she was, she was just as unsure about her and Seth. Where did they stand in all this?

"What about *us?* What happens to us? Will you let your dad and whoever else who wants to, come between us? I'm giving all I possibly can and I want to know that I'm not in this alone. Are you still in this with me? Are we still a couple or...." Seth pulled her close and kissed her passionately on the lips. Shasta fell back against the wall and Seth deepened the kiss. When he stuck his tongue in her mouth, Shasta was prepared to counter and parry. Their passionate interlude went on for endless moments when a car horn broke Seth from trying to make his and Shasta's tongue one and the same.

Shasta looked at Seth a little dazed and was glad to see Seth looked the same way. He smiled at her and kissed her lips once more. He reached into his jean pocket and took out a key ring. He took a small key off the key ring and dropped it into Shasta's open palm.

Shasta looked at the key strangely and waited for Seth to speak. He closed the palm of her hand and gently caressed the soft back of her skin.

"My uncle owns a bed and breakfast on Poppy and Woodland. That key is to the side door. Meet me there at nine tonight. I'll be inside waiting. Just show up at nine." Shasta smiled and nodded. She wanted to talk more but the sound of the car horn told her she had to leave before someone saw them. She looked down at the key in her palm, squeezed it once, kissed Seth one more time and took off running toward her car, anxiously awaiting the evening ahead.

Her thoughts of Laquenta quickly disappeared. She was in deep thought about what was going to happen tonight. She didn't know what to wear or what to expect but she knew one thing for certain, she was going to be with Seth. Vivid flashbacks appeared in her head of them kissing once she got home.

She went straight to her bedroom and laid on the bed. She imagined what it was going to be like lying next to Seth. She wanted him more than ever and couldn't help but feel the warmness in between her legs. She never felt like this before. Was this what love felt like?

She had to get in the shower. She needed to get this feeling out of her system but it wouldn't go away. She held onto herself as the hot water beaded on her back. She bit her bottom lip and whispered Seth's name. She knew she couldn't be too loud because her mother was in the house. She wanted Seth bad and finally she was going to get what they both deserved...each other.

****

She had a surprise visit once she got out the shower. "Shasta...Laquenta is on her way upstairs." Her mother shouted. Shasta's eyes widened because she forgot what she promised Laquenta. Good thing she had information for her.

Laquenta peeked into the doorway but what Shasta was looking at wasn't her old friend. Laquenta had sadness in her eyes and it appeared she'd been crying all day. She quietly sat down on the bed. Shasta was still standing in her towel.

"Hey...don't look so down. I got classified information for you." Shasta smiled as she tried to uplift her friend's spirits.

"What...that Neil is ready to come jumping in my arms?" She asked with an attitude.

"Kinda...sorta. Seth was telling me that Neil's father is abusive. Every time Neil does something wrong he goes and hits his mother. Neil couldn't take that so he took matters into his own hands." Shasta said. She felt accomplished and knew things were going to be better here on out.

"That doesn't explain why he didn't mention anything to me. All he had to do was call and I would have gone along with the plan." Laquenta rolled her eyes. "I don't think he wants to be with me anymore. I can feel it in my soul, besides he hasn't called me or come past my job like he normally would do. I haven't heard from Neil since the day of the party. I can understand what you are trying to do by helping me feel better but the situation doesn't make sense. I think he liked white girls all along and was just curious to see what it was like to be with me." Laquenta paused for a minute before continuing.

"It's so ironic that Neil was so pressed to have sex with me before the party. He was so nice, genuine, and caring. He would kiss me like I was the only woman he cared for…the only woman he loved. And now he won't give me the time or day or talk to me. What kind of mess is that?" She shook her head. "If he really loved me he would have contacted me by now…hell he would have came past my house late one night and throw rocks at my window. He did it before." She scoffed.

"I don't know Laquenta. It does sound fishy to me." Shasta stated. She was still standing in her towel shivering a bit because of the cold draft coming through the window.

"Girl, put some clothes on. Are you afraid to get dressed in front of me?" Laquenta asked.

"You know I'm a little body shy." Shasta mentioned.

"That's because you haven't had sex. Once you do I guarantee you will be walking around naked as much as possible."

"So was Neil your first?" Shasta asked.

"Girl no. I lost mine in high school like normal teens do. Well, unlike you. You're still holding tight for dear life. You don't know what you're missing. I must say Neil had me grabbing bedroom sheets and curling up my feet. I am going to miss that in me but there are other fish in the sea. "

Shasta could tell Laquenta was trying to joke along with her but she couldn't help but feel sorry for her friend. "Hopefully Seth and I will experience that tonight."

Laquenta shot her a look. "What do you mean tonight?"

"He wants to meet with me at the Bed and Breakfast his uncle owns." She replied. She wasn't sure how Laquenta was going to respond but she was seconds away from finding out.

"Be careful...be very careful. I don't want you to end up like me. I know you and Seth care for each other but take what I've just experienced as a lesson. I don't want you to be walking around sad like me." She stared at Shasta with all seriousness. "I know I'm down but I can handle myself. Neil wasn't my first and I know with these good looks he won't be my last but as for you...Seth will be your first and I know you want him to be your last. Just make sure you two are on the same page and will continue to be on the same page once things get rough. I personally think I'm the only person that can and will understand what you're going through. Don't let anyone else know who you are with. I wouldn't even tell your sister if I were you. She wouldn't understand."

"She knows about Seth but she thinks it's a phase."

"And continue to let her think you're in a phase. If she finds out that you two are serious and had sex, it could get ugly. She might mess around and tell your mother and Lord knows how your mother is. I can see her now shutting the community down for a search for Seth."

Shasta took what Laquenta said into consideration. After she got dressed the two of them went to the corner store to have a more in-depth discussion about possible plans for tonight. Shasta was glad she had a friend like Laquenta but was even happier she and Seth were on the same page.

Chapter 18

The street was dark. Shasta parked next to the side door right where Seth told her to. She told her mother she was going over Laquenta's house to stay the night and that she would return after work tomorrow. Her mother was fine with that, since she didn't have to go to work in the morning.

She'd rather have Shasta out of her hair anyway because her new friend was coming over. Momma met a guy at bingo and he'd been pass the house a couple of times. Shasta knew tonight momma was going to want some alone time. This was all perfect timing.

Shasta put the key into the lock and it worked like magic. She was only steps away from being in Seth's arms. Her heart was beating fast and her legs were becoming weak. She knew if Seth was going to kiss her like he did before, then tonight was going to be the night. She bit her bottom lip again as she became aroused. She walked down the dark hallway and noticed one bedroom at the end of the hallway with a dim light. She peered into the door where Seth was lying, waiting for her. A huge smile came across both of their faces.

"Nine o'clock sharp. I love that you're on time." He chuckled.

Shasta walked into the room and quietly closed the door behind her. The moment of spending time with her prince had finally came.

"Don't worry about being quiet…it's just us." Seth assured. "For some reason it's been slow for the past two weeks. I told my uncle I wanted to get away from home since my father and I had been arguing a lot. He's my uncle on my mother's side and they don't care for my father too much. My wish was his command. Come here and let me ease your mind." He said in a sexy tone. It sounded corny but Shasta didn't care, she was living in the moment.

He took off her shoes and laid her gently on the bed. He massaged her shoulders as he passionately kissed her. She kissed him back but this time she was at ease. She didn't have to worry about anyone coming in or seeing them. She was drowning in the fantasy that had become a reality. He put his hands under her shirt and caressed her smooth brown skin. He moved toward her neck and made small circles with his tongue.

Shasta couldn't take it anymore, she quickly unzipped her pants after Seth took off her shirt. He then started kissing her chest and somehow her breast was exposed. She didn't know how it came about nor did she care. Her areolas were sticking out and for the first time a man was looking at them.

"Wow," he gasped. "You're so beautiful," he gazed over her body and looked Shasta deep into her eyes. "I have to have you. I want you, every bit of you,"

She nodded and sighed. He sucked on her breast and the more he did so the wider Shasta's legs got. Her panties were getting soaked from her arousal and she knew this was just the beginning.

She closed her eyes as Seth kissed every inch of her body. She lightly moaned as he got between her legs. She was a bit hesitant when he took her panties off but his soft gentle kisses made her certain her she was in the right hands. She bit her lip as she tried her hardest to refrain from screaming. She was scared and excited at the same time. The sensation of him pleasing her down there was something she could never have imagined. She covered the pillow over her head as she let go of something she couldn't hold any longer. Her body became weak as she shook uncontrollably. She was embarrassed after seeing the results of her release.

"Oh my goodness. I'm so sorry,"

"For what?" Seth said wiping his mouth with his t-shirt. "That was supposed to happen and I am glad it did." He smirked. "You okay?"

"Yes," she gasped. "But what about the sheets, their all soaked." She commented.

"Oh don't worry about that. Here let me put a towel under you. I have more in store."

"You do?" She asked.

"Yes...I do." After putting a towel under her due to the soaked sheets he kissed her again. The feeling came back and Shasta wanted to experience that again, it felt so good and she was now craving for it. She was confident that Seth could make her feel like that again. He sucked her breast again and caressed her body with his hands. Shasta closed her eyes and allowed Seth to take over. She then felt pain that made her open her eyes."What the hell are you doing?"

"Pleasing you." Seth said panting. "Let me please you baby, let me make this night complete."

She didn't understand what he was saying and she was sure he didn't either. He gently placed himself inside of her. She covered her mouth as he hovered over her. He removed her hand and replaced it with his mouth. "Don't worry it will only hurt for a moment," he said in between his kisses. "I don't want to hurt you. After the pain it will feel better. I promise. If not I will kiss it and make it feel all better."

Shasta was scared but she believed him, she relaxed her legs and put then around his waist. She wanted the pain to be over. She couldn't bare it anymore but Seth promised the pain would go away, and it did. Once he got his rhythm going Shasta was enjoying the pleasure she was receiving. She smiled at Seth and even grabbed his chin to kiss her. Her moans were getting louder and the sweat between the two of them was increasing.

After Seth ejaculated they both laid on the bed with exhaustion.

Moments later, Shasta wanted to go again. She wanted to make the best of the night and she was enjoying every bit of it.

****

"What the hell are you doing here?!" An old white man yelled at the top of his lungs, it scared Shasta half to death. Here she was naked under a sheet and a dirty dingy guy was yelling at her for no apparent reason. "This bed and breakfast ain't for no *colored* folks. Get the hell out of my place before I call the cops!"

Shasta was frightened and didn't know what to say. She looked around and noticed she was the only person in the room. *Where the hell was Seth?*

"She's not going anywhere Uncle Joe." Seth replied as he came out of nowhere. He had a tray of food in his hands. It looked as if he was bringing Shasta breakfast in bed.

"You mean this colored whore is with you?"

"She's not a whore, she's my lady!" Seth shouted. "Come on Shasta let's get out of here."

"You have the nerve to bring some colored whore into ***my*** business! Wait until I tell your mother about this. You better find a place to stay because it sure as hell ain't going to be here! Your parents are going to disown you and so am I! If you don't get out of here by the count of three, I'm calling the cops and I'm telling them you broke in here. You and your colored *whore* will be facing jail time." Uncle Joe shouted.

Shasta hurried and put her clothes on once Uncle Joe left the room. She and Seth got into their cars and sped off. She knew she couldn't go home because she told momma she would be back after work. She knew she smelled like sex and couldn't go to work like that. She was flustered and had nowhere to go. Suddenly it came to her that she could go to Laquenta's house.

Seth waved her down,motioning her to follow him. They went to a nearby park that had a bathroom in it. It was too early for anyone to be at the park. Seth knew this was the perfect place for him and Shasta to get dressed.

"Are you okay?" Seth asked getting out of the car after pulling up to the vacant park.

"Yes, he scared the hell outta me," Shasta replied. "Now you're really going to get in trouble."

"Well I might but who cares. I'm with the one I want. I want to be with you and if it means I have to be homeless on the streets then so be it."

Shasta knew from that moment she fell in love with the right man. "Let's go in here and get you all cleaned up. You have to be at work in about two hours right?" He asked.

"Yes."

"Sorry I wanted to feed you but with Uncle Joe and all..."

"I understand." They held hands as they walked to the bathroom. Seth followed her into the ladies room and Shasta already knew what he was thinking.

They kissed and pulled each other's clothes off while in the shower stall. Shasta wrapped her legs around his waist as he thrust himself inside her. Her breasts were in his face and Seth loved every minute of it. He sucked on her breast until he became weak. This time the sex was amazing. She enjoyed every bit of it. She screamed at the top of her lungs from the indescribable pleasure. She loved making love to him. The water ran down both of their bodies as they kissed each other. She didn't want to stop. She would've stayed in the stall for hours if they could have but knew the pleasurable joy ride was over.

Chapter 19

Shasta couldn't stop grinning. She was on cloud nine. She never imagined she could feel this way. Seth had only been gone twenty minutes, yet she ached to be in his arms. Seth. The things he'd done to her body still caused a shiver to go up her spine. Their night together was perfect. It was perfect in every way, except for Uncle Joe. Shasta shook her head. *Why did he have to come in and ruin everything*? Seth had said they would be all alone but now that Uncle Joe knew about them, h*ow long would it be before Seth's parents found out? How long until her mother found out?* Shasta didn't want to think about it. Maybe Uncle Joe wouldn't say anything. He and Seth's dad didn't get along so maybe he would just loathe them from a distance.

Shasta shook her head again. He'd called her a colored whore. No one had ever called her a whore before. She wasn't a whore. She just wanted to be loved, to feel love and to give it back in return. *What was so wrong with that? No one would care if it were a black guy that she was dating. Why did it matter so much because Seth was white?*

All these questions twirled around in her head for endless minutes. She closed her eyes and finished the inventory sheets and made her way to the front. It was slow at the discount store and Debbie stood at the register looking bored. Shasta remembered those days all too well. She was glad about her new position but secretly had to wonder how long she would have it. She was always waiting for the other shoe to drop but so far she hadn't heard from Emily or Ms. Peters since they both were fired. She was nervous and missed Seth but going to be with him was the last thing she could do right now. He told her he was going to the car wash and then going home. She definitely couldn't go to his house and she didn't know where he lived anyway.

Shasta didn't get a chance to talk to Seth about finding an apartment together but maybe she should talk to him about it soon. If her mother found out about them... she knew she didn't want to be around for that. It would not be a pretty sight.

Shasta was still deep in thought when the phone in the back started ringing. She ran to the back to answer it. She answered breathlessly and was about to go into her spiel about the discount store when the voice on the other end cut her off.

"I tried to warn you about giving into Seth too soon and now you'll be learning the lesson of a hard head making a soft behind."

"Laquenta...what are you talking about? You knew I was going to see Seth last night. What happened? Why are you saying this?" Shasta asked gripping the phone and wanting to sit down but her legs wouldn't comply with her mind to coordinate the motion.

"I guess Seth has an Uncle Joe who found the two of you together earlier. Some wild lady came by my job not even half an hour ago, spouting off about some colored whore that's pledged to take her nephew Seth to hell with her in condemnation. She had a Bible in her hand and said it was written in the book of Job that whites could not fornicate with coloreds or they be condemned to hell fire. The whole store was asking who Seth was and who was the girl she was talking about."

"But how did she know to come to your job? How did she know to ask for you?"

"She didn't ask for me. She came in and said that Neil was screwing one of the colored girls there at the store and that we whoring coloreds run together. She wanted a message left for whoever is screwing her nephew and condemning him to hell fire."

"What message is that?" Shasta asked in a whisper, finally seating down in a chair behind the desk.

"She said and I quote, 'Tell the devil's helper we have eyes all over town and she won't escape us. Mark my words.' She left after that and everyone was saying she was crazy. She is crazy but she was dead serious. You and Seth just made a huge step last night but in the light of day, was it really worth all that you can now lose?"

Shasta mulled over what Laquenta had to say most of the morning. By afternoon, she was anxious to see Seth. *He had to know by now what his aunt did right? How long would it be before they found out where she worked and came there?*

Shasta nervously fingered the inventory sheet before grabbing her keys and walking to the front. As she approached, the new girl was ringing up a customer and Shasta leaned in close so only she could hear.

“I’ll be back in a half hour, forty-five tops. If anyone comes in looking for me, tell them that the manager had to step out for a few minutes. Don't give out any more information than that.” When Debbie nodded, Shasta took off and was pulling out of the parking lot in no time. She had to see Seth.

****

When Shasta got to the car wash, she had to park around the corner. She wasn't prepared for the sight she saw and had to cover her mouth to stifle the scream that threatened to escape.

There were close to fifty people walking around with picket signs claiming to end nigger loving. One sign read: 'Nigger whores will not take our good white men.' Another sign read, 'Nigger sluts to the back of the bus' and yet another read,' Lay down with a nigger whore and come up with fleas.' Shasta was devastated. She watched as more people joined the crowd and ducked down in the car. She didn't see Seth at all. *Where was he?*

A man came out with a big amplified speaker and began talking. When Shasta looked closer, she realized the man was Seth's uncle...Uncle Joe. Shasta began crying even before he started shouting to the several dozen bystanders on the pavement.

"Now many of you know my brother in law Billy and know he ain't no saint. And many of you know too the problems I've had with him in the past but this now goes way beyond some crazy disagreements. My crazy nephew has now taken up with a hussy, a whore, and a slut. I saw them myself and can't erase the image from my head. It was disgusting and unimaginable! This is a crime and a travesty. Things like this don't happen in our community. We are the supreme race, not these niggers! We pay our tax dollars and don't rape and steal,these niggers do! They steal everything they can get their hands on and now they're stealing our men. They are taking our white men and casting a devilish spell on them. First Neil, and now Seth! These boys were honor students. Seth was the student body president, now he's fornicating with nigger whores. It's a spell I say. It's the devil coming to destroy us. I say we don't let it happen. I say we take a stand. I say we denounce this before it goes too far. I say we find this nigger whore and teach her a lesson!" The crowd erupted and Shasta was no longer waiting to see Seth at the car wash. She took off at a maddening pace and headed straight to the discount store.

****

"Did you read what was in the paper?" Shasta's mom said during dinner. Shasta had been most of the day. The rally she saw was unreal. *Why was it so hard for two people to be in love with each other?* Shasta didn't know if Seth would pull a Neil on her and date a white girl. She held on to his words hoping and praying they were true. *"We are in this together,"* she kept reminiscing on what Seth said to her at the park. She replayed them making love in the shower, she wanted Seth...she had to be with him now.

"Did you hear me girl?" Her mother questioned.

"Sorry ma, what was in the paper?"

"Girl something has gotten into you. Ever since you started working that new position you have been acting strange. What are they doing to you down there? Those white folks getting to you? You eating they food or somethin'?"

"Ma...no I ain't eating nobody's home cooking but yours. I can't trust anyone."

"Ain't that the truth...well anyways there was a rally at that car wash, you know where all the white folks go. In that nice prestigious community a black person couldn't live there even if they were the mayor." She scoffed.

"Wow the rally was in the paper?"

"Yeah, with a town so small they put everything in the paper. They'll put that a cat was rescued from a tree in the damn paper. People these days...they have nothing better to do. You won't see no black folks doing no rallying. We too busy working and trying to pay these bills. I don't understand how they had the time to do all that! Some man was upset about his nephew dating some black girl. You know anything about that?"

"No." Shasta shook her head quickly. "I couldn't imagine what that was like. I wonder how the couple felt." She stated. She wanted to see what Ma was going to say, she wanted to feel her out and see if she was truly against interracial relationships.

"Girl…ain't no daughter of mine dating no white folk. Could you imagine what the baby would look like, how that baby would be treated and the names it would be called? No, I don't want any of my daughters going through that. That's why I'm so glad your sister married a black man. She has some sense and I know you got em too! Don't you go dating outside your race, not in this day in age. I will not tolerate that. And if any child of mine is dating some white boy, I will disown them. They ain't gonna have the media all at my house in my business. They would tear me apart asking me a million and one questions. That would make the world news!"

"I know Ma, that would be crazy." Shasta agreed. She couldn't tell Ma that the girl they were rallying against was her. She would have no place to go. She needed to talk to Seth as soon as possible. From here on out it would only get crazier. She knew they needed to find a place of their own before she could really be with him.

After dinner Shasta took a shower and laid down. She couldn't stop thinking about what Uncle Joe had called her, *nigger whore* and she started to cry. She couldn't sleep, she had thoughts of them coming to her house and hurting Ma. She knew she couldn't put her family in that situation.

She crept down stairs and got the phone. She called Laquenta hoping she'd pick up. It was only 10:00pm, she knew she wasn't sleep.

"Hello,"

"Hey girl it's me, Shasta."

"Oh hey," she replied dryly.

"What's the matter?"

"Nothing, I'm just tired. I was reading the paper and saw the rally that was at the car wash. I heard Seth's parents wanted him to move to New York when they heard about the two of you."

"Really? I haven't heard from Seth since the day we stayed together."

"And you probably won't hear from him either. Look, I love you and you're a good friend and all but this is getting out of hand. Once they find out where you live or where you work it's over for you. You're going to lose your job and worse of all, you're going to be tortured. They're talking about putting you in jail. I don't know how they gonna do that but you know white folks around here are crazy. His Uncle Joe could make up that you broke into the bed and breakfast and with no proof, they will lock you up." Laquenta stated. "You might as well leave Seth alone and move on with your life while you still can."

"I am not leaving Seth, we are in this together."

"How do you know?" she asked.

"Because, he told me." Shasta said, sounding confident.

"Well, I can't be bothered with you if that happens. I don't want to get in the middle of it. I wish you the best of luck but I have to go..."

"What do you mean you have to go? You're supposed to be my friend." Shasta whispered. She didn't want Ma to wake up and questioned her. She heard the dial tone and knew Laquenta hung up. She didn't want to call back because she didn't want to start any ruckus. *I lost the only friend that understood me. What else am I going to lose?*

Chapter 20

It was late when Shasta snuck out of the house. Momma had fallen asleep on the couch with a Bible in her hand. She had been talking to people all day about what a disgrace the young woman was bringing on her family and her race for dating that so called 'privileged breed'. She knew her Momma's friends were in agreement too. She wanted to cry but she had to see Seth if only for a moment. She had taken a wash cloth and held it in her mouth through most of her Momma's phone conversations. Her mother had no idea she was talking about her own daughter but Shasta had to wonder if it mattered at this point.

She drove around three times and headed toward the park where she first met Seth. It was well after eleven and her face was streaked with tears. *Could this really be happening?* Laquenta had given up on her. She never thought it could be possible. Neil seemed to be totally out of the picture and never looked backward and Seth? She desperately wanted to believe Seth loved her but where was he when she needed him? Had his family made him abandon her? If they had, what would she do? She had never felt so alone in all her life. Not even when her father had died nearly six years ago.

She closed her eyes and tried to think of happier times. She was fourteen years old, her sister had gone on ahead of her at the carnival and was talking to an older cousin of theirs. Her father came up and goose egged her from behind. She was mad at first until she smelled her father's cologne. She smiled and took his hand. He led her over to the cotton candy stand and bought one for her. She loved cotton candy. He had gotten her favorite color too, pink. The flavor was so sweet and the cotton candy was still warm and that made it all the better. She watched as her dad waved to her mother and her Momma came over to stand with them. A man walked by and said he'd take their picture for a dollar and her dad eagerly handed the man the dollar bill. They all posed for the photo and just then, her sister jumped into the photo and made a silly face.

That was a good day. Her family had been so happy. Just four months later, a police officer's stray bullet slammed into her father's chest as he sat at a red light. The bullet went straight through the windshield and hit her dad in the chest as he waited for the light to change. There had been an armed robbery just a few blocks from where her father sat waiting for the light to change. The cop was chasing the suspect on foot and shot an errant shot on a busy street. The suspect was later caught but her father died on the scene. It was two days before her fifteenth birthday.

Shasta was shaken out of her reverie by someone pounding on her window. Her vision was blurry due to the tears but she could make out Seth's form standing by the driver's side window. She opened the door and scooted over to the passengers side.

"Seth, I've been trying to get a hold of you most of the day. Where have you been?" Shasta asked, frantic. Seth actually didn't look so good. He was unshaven and Shasta had never seen him this way.

"I was at the family lakehouse. My dad bought it a few years back but not many people know about it because it was purchased in my name. Everything is just crazy. I heard about the car wash rally. My dad and Uncle Joe nearly went to blows over that demonstration he held...."

"Forget about Uncle Joe, what about us? What are we going to do? All our options just got smaller. We can't go back to the bed and breakfast ever. We can't meet at the car wash. Even if Uncle Joe is banned, your dad can't stop everyone from sneaking around there and my job...I don't know how long it will be before they realize I work at the discount store and then, there goes my job. We have to figure something out."

"I know. I think the lakehouse is the only option but its forty-five minutes from here. We couldn't go there in your car or mine. I got an idea. I have a friend named Ricky that has an old moped. We can use that until we have another solution. I can't see any other way right now." Seth replied and pulled Shasta toward him. Her heart was beating so fast that she thought it was going to jump out her chest and leap right into Seth's arms.

He had a point but she had never been on a moped before. Was it safe? It had to be or Seth wouldn't have suggested it.

"I won't let anything happen to you. All you have to do is hold onto me real tight. I got a helmet that would fit you. Do you want to come with me tomorrow night? We can meet back here but leave your car at home. I walked here tonight but it's really late now. Come at ten. I'll already be here waiting for you." Shasta nodded. Tomorrow night she would be with Seth and she was already making plans to map out their future together.

****

Shasta got home from work; she couldn't wait until it was time for her to leave. She knew she couldn't say anything to Ma but as she approached her home she saw Ma on the porch and she didn't look so happy.

Shasta parked the car and nervously walked up to Ma. "Hey Ma. How was your day?"

"It was good. I'm about to go out and do this rally down the street. Your sister is coming with me. I want you to come with me too." She exclaimed.

"For what Ma? I don't want to get involved in that mess. Why do people care if this random couple wants to be together? It's nobody's business but theirs." Shasta walked pasted Momma and Cassie and made her way to her room. *This is getting out of hand.* She thought to herself.

Ma stayed on the porch and didn't say anything. Cassie rushed upstairs to try and talk some sense into her sister.

"Shasta, you must leave that white boy alone!" She whispered. She watched as Shasta looked in the closet and was skimming through her clothes. "What are you doing?" Cassie asked.

"I'm not leaving him alone, as a matter of fact I'm leaving. And I ain't going to no stupid rally with Ma. Only God knows who's going to be there. Those white people could be down there and I can't risk anyone spotting me. It's bad enough they been rallying all week. I can't be in this house...I don't want to be here. There's no need to live in a community that doesn't accept my decision on who I want to be with."

"Who is going to see you? Those white people are having their own rally. They know not to come down here and start anything with us."

"Ain't no telling, those white people are pissed and I wouldn't be surprised if they did come down here. And if Uncle Joe see me, it's over. I might as well start digging up my own grave, and I don't know about you but quite frankly I'm too young to die!"

"Suite yourself but how are you just going to leave this house? What are you going to say to Ma? If you leave and she can't find you, she's going to get worried, scared and will probably call the cops. She's going to do a missing persons report and when the police find you they're going to see you with that white boy...then what are you going to do?" Shasta didn't think about that.

"Excuse me!" Ma said. She overheard the girls talking. She crept up the stairs when she noticed how quick Cassie followed behind Shasta. The girls didn't know it but Ma was listening to their entire conversation.

"Ma wait!" Cassie said as she stood in front of her sister. She didn't like the decision Shasta was making but she didn't want to see her sister get hurt.

"Oh there's no wait! You mean to tell me you are the one messing with that white boy!" Ma shouted at the top of her lungs. Shasta hoped no one outside overheard her. "How dare you allow the devil inside of you, you probably had sex with the bastard. You are such a slut!" Ma wasted no time as she pushed Cassie out the way and hovered over Shasta. She was hitting Shasta left and right. "Lord get that devil out of her. Get it out of her now!" She screamed.

Shasta's eyes got wide, she didn't know what to do. All she could think of was to go into a fetal position and cover her face with her arms. Ma continued to hit her on her back and pull her hair. Cassie tried her hardest and managed to get Ma off of her sister. Cassie was in tears after she saw what Ma did to Shasta.

"You get out of my house, you get out right now!" Ma screamed. "I'm not having no daughter of mine living under my roof that chooses to mess with the other kind! Do you know what they've put us through? And for you to go and sleep with one of them is a slap in the face. It's a disgrace to your race! How dare you disrespect our ancestors and go and do such a thing?" Momma was standing only inches away from Shasta as Cassie tugged Momma's other arm. She reached her hand in the air and slapped Shasta across her face one last time. Shasta rubbed her face as Cassie pulled Momma away from Shasta.

"I curse the day you were born!" Momma shouted with rage.

Shasta shook her head and disagreed with Momma, "If you don't like what I'm doing, then I will leave. You don't have to worry about seeing me ever again." Shasta responed. She never talked back to Momma. That was something she'd been raised not to do, but tonight all rules were broken. She couldn't hit Momma because she knew she'd die but she wasn't going to leave this house without telling Momma how she felt.

"Come on Ma please...let's just go downstairs." Cassie pleaded. Momma walked backwards toward the door but kept her eyes on Shasta, and Shasta did the same. "Let me tell you something, once you leave this house you are on your own. Don't you come running back to this house. Don't you ever think you have a place to stay here. I don't care if the two of you break up, don't come crying and running back to me."

"You don't ever have to worry about me again." Shasta replied. "Let me tell you something, I love that boy. He's everything to me. He's the only one that has ever listened to me and if I have to get out of your house to be with him, then so be it." Shasta said. She didn't have the energy to scream but she knew by saying what she said sternly, Momma knew she was serious.

"You're a dead girl walking." Momma then turned around and walked down the steps. She heard her sister convincing Momma not to go to the rally. "I know you don't like what she's doing Ma but you can't let people know it's her. You just can't."

"I'm not, I don't have the energy to go. I'm going to take a shower and get in the bed, but I do know one thing, that white loving whore better be out of my house by the time I get out the shower."

Shasta slammed the door, locked it and packed her bags. She knew she had to leave town and tonight had to be the night for that to happen. She was no longer scared about riding on no moped. Her life was in danger and she knew if she didn't leave she would be seeing her father in heaven sooner than she thought.

****

"Put your bags in this compartment here," Seth stated after pulling up to the park. It was dark and Shasta was getting nervous standing at the park alone. She was happy to see him pulling up moments after she arrived at the park.

"Thanks, and I put this on like this right?" She asked as she strapped on the helmet.

"Yes, just like that." He replied. "Hold on to my waist like this and fold your hands together."

Shasta looked at the moped and was a bit hesitant to get on. "It's okay, I promise I will not let you get hurt. You can trust me right?" He asked.

"Yes, I can trust you." She allowed Seth to help her on the moped after he got on. But before she did, she wanted a kiss. If she was going to die tonight at least she'd get a kiss before she met her maker.

Kissing Seth wasn't something she wanted to stop doing. She wanted to go back into the bathroom and make love again, but she knew time was not on her side. She figured they'd make love all night like they did at the bed and breakfast once they got to the cabin.

She jumped at the sound of the moped when Seth turned it on. It let a little kickback that frighten her but as Seth promised, nothing bad happened. She laid her head on his back as he guided them to their destination. She replayed the look on Ma's face when she overheard Cassie talking about her and Seth.

She knew she and Cassie weren't real close but she was glad her sister was there to protect her from Ma trying to beat her to death. When Shasta left she overheard Ma crying in her room. She couldn't imagine how she felt at that moment. She overheard Ma talking: *They are going to kill my baby. Lord why did you allow her to like a white boy...that's not right Lord...that's not right.*

Cassie warned her that it would be best if she did leave. She didn't approve of her being with a white boy but Shasta believed a part of her sister understood how she felt. *You can't help who you love, but society wouldn't see it like that,* were the words her sister last said to her. Shasta remembered running out the house and not looking back. She was going to miss her sister and Ma but her life was in danger and there was no reason to turn back now. She chose her love life over her family and if no one was going to understand that, then fleeing town was the best decision her and Seth could make together.

Chapter 21

It was well after midnight when the folks began to file in two and three at a time into the Brown house. The rally was over for now but many had noticed Mrs. Brown was MIA and had come to check up on her. A few of the ladies from the church poured in and some of Mrs. Brown's closest friends. Mrs. Brown directed all the women to join hands and began to pray. It wasn't long into the prayer that Mother Tucker began to shoot out the Lord's name. As Mrs. Brown finished her prayer, Mother Tucker turned to her with understanding and fear in her wide set brown eyes.

"The girl they looking for is your girl Shasta, ain't it?" Many of the women were shaking their head and looking for Mrs. Brown to deny the charge but Mrs. Brown could only shake her head and ring her hands.

"You see this. This girl has her mother so upset that she can't even answer. What has gotten into her? The devil I say! This child was an innocent but innocent she is no longer! Lord please cast this demon out of dear Shasta. Lord she was brought up in the church. She knows you dear Lord. Please deliver her. Deliver Sister Brown, deliver all of us. We need you Lord. We call on you in the midnight hour. Renew our strength, Lord! The devil has taken one of your children Lord. Bring her back! Bring her back dear Lord...."

“I don't want her back. She made her choice. She's twenty-one now. She made her bed, now let her lie in it.” Mrs. Brown said sitting down.

“Martha, you don't mean that. You love your daughter. We all know you do. You're upset right now, you're angry but...”

“You’re damn right I'm upset but I'm way past that right now. She has been defying everything I have taught her for months. Cassie was reluctant to tell me but Laquenta had a white boyfriend and then Shasta wanted one too. There's no telling how many times she snuck out to meet him pretending to be hanging out with Laquenta. When Laquenta's so called boyfriend left her high and dry, Shasta should've learned but no! She only wanted to be with that white boy even more. I called Laquenta's parents and they made her get on the phone and tell me the whole story. All of it. She was right to distance herself from the situation and now I'm following suit.”

“Martha, this is Mother Tucker here. I know you love that girl. You don't mean what you say. You're upset and with good reason but you can't turn your back on your child. You just can't. The Lord will not condone such behavior.” Mother Tucker said and sat down beside her.

"Well, I'm sorry Mother Tucker but this is my cross to bear with God and He has my back. Shasta should have made sure He had her back too because if those white folks find her, she's gonna need more than me on her side. I already told her I'm through with her. I'll pray for her safety but beyond that, I can't and won't do anymore. She's on her own."

****

Shasta tipped out of bed and went downstairs. Seth was sound asleep and for that she was thankful. Barely an hour after they got to the lake house, they were in each other's arms and making sweet love. She blushed as she recalled getting on top of Seth and grinding her hips deep into his pelvis. It felt so good. It felt so right. The love they felt for each other wasn't wrong was it? Everyone around them said it was. Even down to her own mother. Her mother. Why had she thought of her? It was nearly three in the morning but she bet her Momma was still up and she bet she wasn't alone either.

The women of the church were probably surrounding her and telling her what a devil child she had for a daughter. Shasta almost laughed to keep from crying, almost. She had nowhere to go. She was here with Seth but how long could they stay there before they were on the run again. What if Seth decided he didn't want to keep running, what would they do? There were so many questions racing through her head.

She loved Seth, she really did but he clearly had way more options than she did. They didn't want his head on a silver platter like John the Baptist, only hers. For the first time in months, she dropped to her knees and prayed to the Lord for an answer of what to do next.

****

"Hey are you okay? I saw you on the floor. Why are you down here and not in bed?" Seth had came downstairs, startling Shasta. She was trying to pray and realized she was doing a terrible job of it. She wanted an answer right away and remembered her Momma saying that God doesn't work like that. Then she tried to start over and was still asking for God to help her right now and take all her pain away. She couldn't remember the prayer her father taught her and she had started to cry. That's when Seth had come downstairs.

Seth walked over to her and lifted her to her feet. He felt her tremble and pulled her close to him. Once she wasn't shaking so much, he asked her again what she was doing on the floor.

"I was praying. I was trying to anyway. God probably isn't listening to me though."

"I think prayer is okay, I guess. My parents don't go to church. I think my mom believes there's a God but my dad says he's a self made man and don't believe in God. He says it's all nonsense."

"What about you? What do you believe?" Shasta asked, resting in Seth's arms.

"I don't know. Something *is* in the universe. I get that. I know that many people die and many people are born. They say that's the purpose under heaven but beyond that, I think we are moving to the beat of our own drum." Shasta listened but didn't really know what to think of Seth's answer. That was just one more thing that proved how different they were. Shasta *knew* God existed. She had just forgotten how to connect with him. She closed her eyes now and asked God to protect them because only *He* knew how in over their heads they really were.

******

When Shasta woke up, it was nearly 9 o'clock in the morning. She couldn't believe she had slept so long, if you call what she was doing sleeping. She was so restless. Seth had kneaded her shoulders and set her body at ease but her mind was like a wild race horse. *Would this feeling of nauseousness ever end?* Her family had forsaken her. Her best friend was gone and she knew she would soon be out of a job. *What was next?*

When she finally was able to focus her eyes, she realized Seth was out of the bed. Where was he at? She didn't want to panic but she could just envision Uncle Joe busting in with a twelve gage shotgun cocked, loaded and aimed at her chest. Oh hell naw! She jumped from the bed and raced down the stairs. She got to the bottom of the stairs and heard Seth talking. *Who was he talking to this early in the morning?* She walked over to the window and pushed back the curtain...

Shasta wasn't sure who this person was Seth was talking to. Her heart jumped when she realized the person was in uniform, it looked as if the person was a cop. Seth appeared to be in deep conversation and Shasta knew it would be in her best interest to stay put. She didn't want to make any noise. *Did the person think they were trespassing? She* and Seth already had the community searching for them, she couldn't risk getting caught and going to jail or worse.

She tiptoed to the bathroom and sat on the toilet. She rocked herself back and forth anticipating what was going to happen next. She closed her eyes and said a prayer. "Lord...watch over me...watch over us," she whispered. She tried hard to listen to what was being said but she made it harder for herself when she walked into the bathroom. She heard voices but couldn't make out what they were saying. Soon the voices faded and there was a slight knock on the door.

"It's me Shasta." Seth warned.

She quickly got up, straighten out the t-shirt she wore to sleep. It was actually Seth's t-shirt, it was two sizes too big but she loved it because his scent was on it. She opened the door with a worried look on her face.

"Everything is okay," He replied. "That was just the ranger. He wanted to know if I had papers proving I was a resident here. I remember Mom always putting the residential papers in the desk by the kitchen. I showed it to him and he was relieved. He said a few weeks ago someone tried to break into another cabin just a mile away from this one. He said he does checks in the mornings and when he noticed the moped outside he got suspicious. Good thing I was here when he knocked on the door, otherwise he probably would have contacted my parents to make sure they were up here on vacation and not some burgular ."

"Oh really." Shasta was relieved. She'd done enough running for one day. She wasn't ready to get back on the road.

"Yeah. It looks like we're safe here. We can rest for a couple of days and figure out what we are going to do from here on out."

"I think we should leave the state, possible go up north to Maryland...Pennsylvania, or...."

"Wait, how about New York? How would we get there though?" Seth asked cutting Shasta off. He looked at Shasta intently. Her eyes became massive. She was ready to see what the world was like outside of Virginia. There was nothing but crazy racism there.

"The moped...or we can catch the long distance bus or something. We don't have to act like we're together."

"How am I supposed to act like I'm not with you?" Seth asked as he crept his hand up Shasta's t-shirt.

"Oh I believe once we leave here we can play the part." She giggled knowing what was about to happen. Her plan this morning was to make breakfast and feed her man but it appeared there was going to be a delay in making that breakfast.

Seth placed Shasta on top of the bathroom sink and took her shirt off. He loved looking at Shasta's body, her smooth caramel skin stunned him every time he laid his eyes on her body. He kissed her on the lips and made his way down her chest. He stopped for a detour and Shasta enjoyed every bit of it. She didn't want to leave the cabin. She wanted to remain in Seth's arms as long as she could.

Chapter 22

Shasta went down to the lake and looked out over the huge expanse of land. Seth's family had a lot of land. She supposed they would call it an estate. All of her family's houses were so close together that if Aunt Bertha sneezed or coughed, Uncle Raymond could yell 'God bless you' from the next house over. Here no one could hear you for miles unless they were already on the property. It was eerily quiet. Shasta wasn't used to such silence.

Seth had fallen asleep after round two of their lovemaking romp and truthfully, Shasta was tired too but she just couldn't rest. It was late afternoon and she decided to head back to the house. She sat down on the comfortable tan sofa and leaned her head back. She allowed her body to rest a moment and picked up the remote on the table.

She looked at it for a moment before pressing the power button. When she looked at the screen, she wasn't surprised to see the color of the tube. She didn't have a colored TV at home and when they wanted to change the channel, her or Momma had to get up and turn the dial. Her eyes widened as she realized it was the first time she had seen any TV in color. She was in awe. She watched half of All in the Family and turned the channel.

She didn't know the stations there and after a minute or two of channel surfing, she settled on the news. She wished she hadn't. There on the set was a demonstration going down at the bed and breakfast where she had met up with Seth. Again Uncle Joe and his ugly wife were right in the thick of it. Many of the crowd members had signs that read 'Whites Only', No Nigger Lovers Allowed Here, and 'Stand Up and Proclaim Our Race'. Shasta watched on in horror as one man held up a picture of Rosa Parks and proceeded to pee on it as the crowd egged him on.

A cop came over to admonish the man but the two then shared some unheard joke causing them both to bust into laughter. The news cameras zeroed in on a woman carrying a headless black naked, baby doll. On the doll's body the words 'Satan's spawn' was written in permanent maker. Shasta had to turn away. Why did they hate her kind so? No one ever messed with any of those people that she saw rallying there at the bed and breakfast. Her people were the ones struggling. Her people were the ones hungry. Her people were the ones with no jobs or housing. Not these ungrateful bastards.

As the tear drops began to fall, Shasta knew in her heart what she wanted to do but wondered if she even had the courage to go through with it. She loved Seth, she really did but someone had to take a stand. She just hoped she had the strength and determination to pull it off without getting herself killed in the process.

Three days later, Shasta went down to the river. Seth had left to go get some supplies and had been gone for nearly a half hour. She didn't really know how much time she had before he got back so while he was napping, she brain stormed. She had to get a message to Cassie somehow. Laquenta had given up on her but Cassie still loved her. Cassie would help her out when no one else would. She just knew it.

Shasta searched until she found an old mailbox at the end of the street. As she looked closer, she realized that there were two mailboxes close together. One read Swilling and the other read Avery, which Seth's last name. She made a quick decision and put the letter in the mailbox that read Swilling. She didn't know if Seth would check the mail or not and didn't want him to find the letter. It had been so long since she had sent a letter off so she didn't know if the stamp she found in one of the drawers was current. She prayed it was.

As Shasta hurried back to the house, she prayed Cassie would not say anything to Momma. She had left specific orders not say a word to Momma or anyone else in the family. It wasn't so much that she didn't want anyone to know where she was. She didn't want anyone to know what she was about to do. Cassie wouldn't like it but she had to do something. She was sick of feeling like the underdog.

Everyone was afraid to speak up. Momma was afraid. The church members were afraid, Laquenta was afraid.

The masses were afraid. Shasta was scared too but if everyone just sat idly by and did nothing, these people would win. They had been winning for years. People like Uncle Joe, Seth's dad and Aunt had been the needle that was breaking the camel's back for years. The time was now to show them that blacks had someone who would stand up for them and Shasta felt like she was just the one to show them. She knew the Reverend Jesse Jackson was head and founder of the PUSH Coalition and felt that he was just the ammunition she needed to drive her point home.

****

"Is everything okay?" Seth asked as he walked into the house. He had a couple of bags in his hand as he maneuvered his way into the kitchen.

"Yes, but I was thinking...I don't think we can stay here much longer. It's only a matter of time before your family think to come here and search for us."

"I know and I think you're right. That's why I bought a few things. I have a flashlight, some perishable foods, some sweaters and a blanket. I think we could use it for the cold nights. I want to prepare myself as we make our way up to New York." Seth looked at Shasta for a happy response and he got just that.

Shasta jumped out of her seat and kissed him on the lips. "We need to leave tonight. I was watching the news and it was confirmation for me…we have to go." She insisted.

"No worries, we will do just that. I just have to figure out how to get to New York."

"Just go the road. We should find it one way or another. And if we don't end up in New York, it doesn't matter. As long as we got each other…"

"We should be fine," Seth said finishing her sentence.

"Let's pack a suitcase and clear things out so that people won't know we were here." Shasta suggested.

They did just that. Shasta had a funny feeling that if they didn't leave tonight, it would be the last night they spent together. Her heart was beating a thousand miles a minute. Just something on the news got to her. She didn't want to get caught because if she did, she knew death would be right around the corner.

Chapter 23

"I want you to run out to the woods as fast as you can." Seth said shaking Shasta out of her sleep. They decided to take a nap before leaving to go on their journey, but things were ruined by the sound of someone banging on the door.

"I know you're in there!" A voice cried out, it sounded like someone Seth knew.

"On second thought, climb out the window and hide in one of the trees. I'm going to try to dodge whoever is at the door." He whispered.

Shasta wanted to cry but she knew that wasn't going to solve anything. She did as she was told and climbed out the window. There was a branch she was able to climb on with the help of Seth after she got on the roof. She went up on the tree and studied herself. It was a good thing she wore black because no one was able to see her.

She climbed as high as she could so that she could see the front of the house. She noticed a woman standing out front talking to Seth. She tried hard to listen and stayed as quiet as possible.

"What's going on? What are you doing here?" The neighbor asked. She was a close friend of the family. Seth had to play it cool otherwise she could ruin it for him and Shasta.

"I just came up here to get away." He replied nonchalantly.

"I saw you on the news, so is it true? You messin' around with one of those black girls?" She questioned.

Seth sighed. "No, not anymore. That's why I wanted to get away from all of the madness. My parents ordered me to stay away from her. We went our separate ways and now I'm out here trying to heal. My parents or anyone would understand."

"Is that right? What makes her special anyways? What could she do that us pretty white girls couldn't?"

"It's hard to explain. I mean, the girl was something special." Seth said trying to get rid of the nosy neighbor.

"Right. Well, your mother thought you were up here. She told me to come and see if you were home. She's coming first thing in the morning, so I wanted to warn you before you got all surprised. You sure you don't want me to come in and help you get over your ol' friend?" She asked rubbing his shoulder. Shasta immediately got mad but she was glad the stupid bimbo gave them what they needed to know.

"It's cool. I think it's best my parents come up here. I was beginning to wonder how I was going to get back home." He chuckled. He didn't want the neighbor to know about the moped they had in the back of the house.

"Well it's your lost, take care of yourself. It was nice to see you again. Maybe when you get over that girl of yours, you can come get with a real winner."

"I will keep that in mind, goodnight Kim." Seth closed the door and Shasta knew he was on his way back upstairs.

She met him back in the room, "A real winner, ha?" Shasta joked.

"Oh please, don't get me started. She's liked me since I was ten years old. She gave me some good information though."

"Yeah, your folks are coming up here in the morning. How'd she know you were here?"

"The lights were on. I take it her family is up here on vacation. I mean it is summer time and this is around the time they come up here. I'm so glad she came knocking on the door, otherwise if someone saw you, it would have been a lot worse. Let's get our things together now and head up north."

Shasta listened to Seth and they did just that. It was a little after one in the morning when they left. They knew everyone would be asleep, even his nosy neighbor

Kim. Shasta clutched onto the back of Seth's jacket and enjoyed the ride to their next destination.

A lot of things were going through her head. She wondered if her sister was ever going to get the letter, or if Momma was going to be nosy since the letter went to her house. She couldn't remember Cassie's address by heart so she prayed Momma at least let Cassie read it. She then remembered leaving her scarf on the table in the living room. She knew his mother was going to find it and automatically suspect that she was there.

She didn't know how long she was going to be able to run. She continued to think about her and Seth getting caught. She knew this was going to make the national news. People all over the east coast was going to be looking out for them. And who's to say their relationship would be accepted in New York? What if when they get there they were treated way worse? Should they make their way to Canada? Shasta was confused and she surely wasn't certain what Seth would do if they hit a dead end. What if he was forced to chose, would he stay with her or was his life more important than their love?

A few tears rolled down Shasta's cheeks. All she wanted to do in life was to find love. She never would have thought loving someone that society didn't accept would make her life turn into a living hell.

****

As Seth pulled over at the gas station to refuel, Shasta looked around. They were in New York. She was both excited and nervous. Would they be able to make it here? Would they be accepted or shunnned? Seth would be the key. She had never traveled away from home but she was sure this was not foreign to Seth. The way he responded from here on out would make or break their relationship.

Shasta was deep in thought when she realized Seth had been calling her name. She blushed and turned her gaze to his. "What were you so deep in thought about? You aren't afraid are you? I told you I won't let anyone hurt you." Seth said and pulled her toward him.

" I know, it's just nerves I guess. I've never been here before. It seems so fast paced. The women are wearing bell bottom jeans and halter tops. You don't see that in Virginia." Shasta said, again looking around.

" I guess it will take a bit to get used to all of this but at least we are here together." Shasta nodded and rested her head on Seth's shoulder. Two passerbys looked their way and stared at them long and hard but said nothing as they continued on to the gas station. Shasta exhaled and sighed. Finally they were somewhere that the color of their skin didn't matter.

It took them two days to get to New York because they stopped to rest as often as they could and was watchful of strangers on the road. Shasta no longer found herself worried about if Cassie got the letter she sent to Momma's house. Maybe Momma saw her handwriting and just threw the letter away. If seemed like she didn't need Reverend Jackson's help after all. She and Seth would make it without anyone's help.

She smiled a genuine happy smile for the first time in days. She and Seth left the gas station and headed east toward a diner called Taste of Home. Seth said the gas station clerk told him the food was really good there. Shasta had to admit she was starving. It was well after 4 when they had stopped to get gas and it was just after 4:30 when they pulled into the diner.

The diner appeared to be packed if the cars outside were any indication. Once they walked in, Shasta went straight toward the restroom to freshen up some. A few minutes later, she joined Seth at the booth in the corner. Seth smiled at her as she sat down. She smiled back. It took her a minute to realize that they had a captive audience. Nearly half the diner was staring at their table. There were a few blacks in the diner. One man sat at the counter alone, another man sat at a nearby table pretending to be reading the paper and there was one male washing dishes in the back.

Shasta suddenly felt nervous. Was it a good idea to come here? No one said a word which made it even harder to read them. Seth seemed okay with everyone staring at them but was he really? Shasta didn't know if she would ever get used to the feeling.

She saw a glass of iced tea placed in front of her and was glad Seth had ordered it. She was thirsty. She took a huge swallow and set the glass down. A female waitress approached to take their orders.

"What'll you have?" Betsy asked and took the pencil from behind her ear. She asked the general question to both of them but she only looked toward Seth for an answer. Seth must have already had it figured out because he asked for two of the house specials which turned out to be tuna melts on wheat with french fries. Shasta didn't say anything. She had never had a tunamelt before or had ever eaten wheat bread. She hoped she liked it. The specials were $2.99 a piece. She knew Seth didn't have a lot of money and she had zero. She had a check for about $140 wanting for her in Virginia but she wouldn't be going back there to get it. She had to get a job in New York. So did Seth. It was the only way they would make it.

They talked for a bit about checking into a hotel and then early the next morning, they would both hit the pavement hard in search of a job. The waitress returned with their food and they started to eat. Shasta ate a few of the fries and drank more of the iced tea. She began to sample her sandwich and instantly felt nauseous. Seth was already done with one half of his sandwich so Shasta took a few more bites of the tuna melt but found that she really didn't like it all that much. She munched away on her fries and the waitress came over to refill Seth's coke and took her iced tea glass to refill it as well. Shasta took a long swig with her straw. The tea was so good and cold. Shasta was nearly done with her fries when someone turned up the volume on the TV. She was reaching for her glass when she heard a voice she would never forget if she lived to be a hundred years old. The volume wasn't real high but she was spell bound as she watched the television and couldn't move.

“I've asked for deliverance for my child. She's a marked woman now. I tried to tell her that being with that boy would do her no good. I begged her to leave him be! Now my big girl is in the hospital and may never wake up and all because of a hate crime. All because my youngest child wouldn't listen and stay away from a boy that will never truly love her. I asked why did it have to be my child who stepped out on faith, religion, creed and her own kind. Why mine? I've serviced the Lord faithfully, buried one husband shot down and killed. She knows that! She's scandulous because only what's between her legs matters most to her now. Not me, not her sister! Not the people who helped raised and comforted her. No. We no longer matter. I ask that you deliver my child. She knows not what she's doing. She never would have let her sister be put in a coma if she was in her right state of mine. Lord please deliver my child cause only you can take hold of her now." Someone came over to take the mic away from her Momma and some white woman was holding up a sign that read "Protect the white race from the devil's nurse maids." Shasta looked away as tears rolled down her cheeks. Cassie was in the hopsital? Was it because of her? Momma had said it was. Oh God, what had she done?

Chapter 24

Shasta awoke with a start. She almost forgot where she was. Seth was already gone and looking for work. She had to find a job. Cassie and Momma came to mind. Both were in so much pain and she could no longer kid herself that she wasn't the cause of it. She knew where the blame lay and that was at her feet.

She went into the bathroom and took a quick shower. It was after ten when she got dressed. She rushed out of the hotel room and was on Lafeyette in no time. She crossed her fingers and prayed she wouldn't strike out. Seth was counting on her and more importantly, she had something to prove to herself.

By noon Shasta was tired and thirsty. She had bombed out at every place she tried to apply. Even shop owners with help wanted signs in the window were telling her that the position had been filled. She walked block after block and nothing. She had fifty cents in her pocket and came across a diner with a small red and blue sign that read 'Faygo pop twenty-five cents'. She rushed in the diner and took a seat near the door. It was a black owned restaurant. There were pictures of Martin Luther King on the wall,Aretha Franklin, Gladys Knight and Sammie Davis Jr. Despite all her angst, she felt instantly at home.

A young waitress came over to take her order. She told her she just wanted a Faygo red pop. The girl nodded and left to go get it. Shasta looked around again. Soft Rhythm and Blues played in the back ground and a small color TV was mounted to the wall. She closed her eyes and hummed as Smokey Robinson belted out a few notes. She opened them a few moments later as she realized someone had been calling to her. It was the man from the diner from the night before.

"I didn't think I'd see you again. Are you stalking me?" Shasta blinked, then realized he was joking. He had kind eyes and was handsome as all get out. She *did* remember him. Who wouldn't. He was tall, handsome and had some of the prettiest brown eyes she had ever seen. She blushed despite herself and realized he had brought out the red Faygo to her. She quickly snatched up the bottle and took a several gulps. She wasn't surprised to see Mr. Gorgeous smiling down at her.

"You were thirsty huh?" All Shasta could do was nod. She was thirsty. The bottle was more than half gone already. She looked at Mr. Gorgeous and realized she hadn't paid for her drink. Was that way he still hovered over her? She dug into her pocket and pulled out the quarter. He wanted his money. She was sure more now than ever that he was the diner's owner.

" This is for the pop. I didn't mean to seem like I wasn't gonna pay or anything." Shasta looked startled as Mr. Gorgeous started chuckling.

"No worries honey. Your money is no good here but if you want to give that quarter to my cousin Antoinette, it's entirely up to you." Mr. Gorgeous walked away and went off toward the back of the diner. Shasta strained her neck to see where he'd gone off to but she didn't see him anywhere and he never came back to the front of the diner. She could hear him talking softly to a woman and every now and then, the woman would let out a girly giggle. Who was he and what did he mean that her money was no good here?

She pondered all of it sitting at the table by the front door for endless minutes before realizing she had more than stayed her welcome. She got up to leave and before she opened the door, she looked toward the back to see if she saw Mr. Gorgeous but he was nowhere insight. She pushed through the heavy door and walked out into the hot Summer air, never realizing Mr. Gorgeous was watching her all along.

****

By the time Shasta made it back to the hotel room, it was just after six o'clock. She had struck out at every turn. No one showed the slightest interest in hiring her. All the positions were filled her or they no longer needed help but forgot to take down the help wanted sign. She knew what it was. Many of these same people she was asking to hire her had seen her with Seth when they rode into town. Not even in New York was she being cut a break.

She was about to take off her blouse and put on a t shirt when Seth burst through the door beaming. It was obvious he was happy about something. She looked in his hand. He had money. It looked like a bunch of dollars but he had cash. Where had he gotten it?

"Honey, I'm home." Seth said, laughing and fell back onto the bed. Shasta tossed her blouse and put on the t shirt. She climbed on the bed and peered down at Seth. Had he robbed a bank? Oh no, there wasn't enough cash there for a bank robbery. Maybe a corner store or bar. Oh no! They were going to jail for sure. Momma would be even farther disgraced if possible. They had to leave and leave now. Shasta jumped off the bed and started packing. Seth got up off the bed to still her movements.

"Hey, what are you doing? Why are you packing?"

"Do you really have to ask? They will be here soon to take us to jail and for what $30? I think we better run before they track us down here." Shasta said turning away and stuffing they blouse and a pair of shorts in the knap sack. Seth spun her around and stilled her hands again.

"What do you mean they will be coming after us? Who? My parents, your family, who?"

"The police that's who. We gotta get outta here. Thirty dollars may pay for this hotel room for a few nights but I ain't going to jail over it." Shasta went into the bathroom to pack up her few toiletries and came back out to the where Seth lay laughing on the bed. She set the knap sack down and jumped on the bed. Seth had lost his cotton pickin' mind. What the hell was wrong with him? Didn't he see the urgency? Apparently he was a fickle as he was handsome.

"Oh my God, you think I stole the money don't you?" Seth finally asked after cracking up for over a minute. Shasta thought it was obvious. Of course he had. How else did he get that money?

"Yes, and we better start moving or we are gonna be dead fishes in water and..."

"I earned it at work." It was all Seth said as he turned on the TV. Shasta just looked at him, and then reality dawned on her, somewhat anyway.

"You got a job?" Shasta asked and leaned against the wall.

"Sure did. Left bright and early and the second guy I met was in need of a dock worker and hired me on the spot. Been working since about nine this morning. Got fourty bucks too. I couldn't believe my luck...." Seth went on and on but every word seemed to fade in the background for Shasta. She had really beat the pavement today. She had been to shop after shop and store after store walking. At least Seth had taken his moped and he had gotten hired after just his second job inquiry. It wasn't fair. She sat down on the bed and half listened as Seth told her that the money he had gotten was just an advancement. Advancement? She never heard of it. Blacks didn't get advancements, they got kicked in the teeth and for the first time in a long time, she realized just how different she and Seth really were.

****

A few hours went by and Shasta looked out the window gazing at the sky. She could barely see anything since the tall buildings were in the way, yet she couldn't let go of the fact that Seth got a job after looking for only a few hours.

"What do you want for dinner?" Seth asked, interrupting her thoughts. He stretched his arms in the air and his body became limp after a good few hours of rest.

"It doesn't matter, whatever you want to eat." She replied, not wanting to show any frustration.

"I was thinking of a pizza since it's pretty cheap. I want to be smart with my money. I know we're going to be looking for a place soon but I want to make sure I have enough for it."

"Right."Shasta said and Seth reached out for a hug before he walked out the room. "See you in a bit."

Shasta nodded. *My money,* was the only word that stuck in her head. She was concerned about how things were going to play out in the near future. What if she didn't get a job and Seth got tired of taking care of the both of them? Would he kick her out and send back to Virginia? Shasta wasn't sure what was going to happen. One thing she knew for certain was that people acted funny when it came to money, no matter what the color of their skin was.

All of a sudden she remembered the place she went to, the black owned diner. She knew that place was her only chance, but if they found out her boyfriend was a white boy, what would happen then? She was starting to think her chances of making it in New York wasn't as easy as she expected it to be. She laid down on the bed , pondering on the decisions she had to make. The last thing she wanted was to get all the way to New York and be stranded. That wasn't going to happen, there was no way in hell Seth was going to leave her hanging.

Chapter 25

Seth was up early the next morning but Shasta was too. Seth showered quickly and stuffed his face full of the last slice of pizza in the pizza box before dropping a quick kiss to her check and heading out the door. He had tried to open up her cookie jar last night after he brought back the pizza but Shasta pretended the pizza had given her heart burn. She was still so frustrated. It had been so easy for Seth to get a job but she had practically gotten the door slammed in her face at every step. Except... Shasta showered and dressed quickly. Maybe, just maybe, she had a shot after all.

By the time Shasta got to the diner, it was a quarter after nine. It had taken her forever to go seven blocks. There were way too many people in New York for her taste. When she got to the diner, she realized the it didn't open until ten o'clock. She decided to go up the street and sit on the bench. It was another scorcher today. It was burning up already. She reached into her pocket and realized she still had the two quarters from the day before. She smiled a wry smile. 'Your money is no good here.' Why had he said that and why was he being so nice? No one else was. Not really anyway. She fully intended to find out and ten o'clock couldn't come fast enough.

At ten o'clock on the nose, Shasta stood outside the diner, preparing to go inside. She could see a few customers already sitting at tables. Had she read the sign wrong? She looked again. It read Open ten to eight Monday through Saturday. Open one o'clock to seven Sundays. Closed Wednesdays. She blinked once and opened the door. She instantly inhaled. How hadn't she noticed the sweet smells yesterday? She was definitely noticing them today. Hmm. Sweet potato pies, candied yams, collard greens, dressing, macaroni and cheese, baked chicken, turkey, sweet maple ham... she was reading the menu on the wall and could feel her mouth start to salivate. She could feel her palms get moist and she rubbed them down her skirt, pretending to smooth it out.

She saw the waitress from the day before. What was her name? Antoinette. She was busy with a couple and hadn't noticed her. Shasta instantly dug into her pocket and fished out one of the quarters. She didn't pay the day before and suddenly she realized that if Mr. Gorgeous came out, she could use the Faygo pop as an excuse.

As you would know it, Mr. Gorgeous did come out with a tray heaping with delicious goodies and was heading toward her. He stopped but for a second but quickly spun around and flawlessly delivered the party of three their meals that were sitting in a booth. Shasta hadn't seen them when she first came in but her gaze was fixated there and it had nothing to do with the patrons or the booth. Mr. Gorgeous finally lifted his gaze and looked directly her way. He started walking toward her but Antoinette returned with the couples drink orders and he took them from her. He whispered something in her ear and Antoinette turned and looked her way. She nodded and went off toward the kitchen.

Shasta didn't have to wait long for Mr. Gorgeous to come seek her out. She had barely sat down near the door when he came and took the seat right across from her. Shasta gulped. She hadn't expected that. She reached into her pocket and pulled out the quarter. She would use the quarter as a scapegoat. It would be the reason she came.

"I never paid yesterday. I brought this back. It's for the Faygo." Shasta set the quarter on the table. She finally got the nerve to look up at Mr. Gorgeous. She nearly fainted. What she saw in his eyes, she had never seen in Seth's. It was understanding, it was admiration, it was sensitivity and something else. It was the something else that she wanted to know more of.

"I'll tell you today like I told you yesterday, your money is no good here. I think you heard me loud and clear yesterday. So why don't you tell me the real reason you have come back." Shasta couldn't believe how well he had read her. It was a little startling and exciting all at the same time. If he wanted the truth, she'd give it to him. Half of it anyway.

"I did come back to pay for the Faygo pop but I really came back because I need help." And to see you but Shasta kept the last part to herself. Mr. Gorgeous seemed to mull over the last bit of information she gave him and leaned back in his chair.

"Help with what, what are you in need of?"

"I'm in need of a job. Can you help me out? Do you know anyone around here that's hiring? I'll do just about anything as long as it's legal." Mr. Gorgeous had sat up and was listening to her intently but before she finished her spiel, he had again leaned back in his chair. He scratched a spot just above his eyebrow that had Shasta transfixed.

"Well, I can say that today is your lucky day. I have just the job offer for you."

****

Shasta had to be hearing things. Had Mr. Gorgeous said he had a job for her? No, he couldn't have. She had been so caught up in his beautiful eyes that her ears were playing tricks on her.

"What did you say? I thought you said you had a job for me."

"You heard me right. I do have a job for you. My cousin will be starting school early next week but if you can be here tomorrow morning by ten o'clock...."

"I can, I can." Shasta exclaimed and had to silently count to five to calm down. She didn't want to blow this. The thought of working with him made her blood boil. She had never felt this way before.

"Okay, I will personally be giving you the tour of the diner. My Cousin Becky is the cook and you will be helping her with prep initially. After a few days, I'll show you the ropes on the floor. There are only three waitresses that work here and I help fill in when needed. I'm pretty hands on so I wait tables too if there's a rush and weekends are always busy here." Shasta smiled despite herself. What was it about him? He was *FINE,* and he awed her in ways Seth didn't but there was something else. She was anxious to get started but tomorrow would be soon enough. Her head was dizzy with excitement. She finally had gotten a job.

"Does that sound okay to you?" It took a minute to sink in that he was talking to her again and all she could do was nod. When Mr. Gorgeous went to walk away, she finally found her voice. When she spoke, she wished she hadn't.

"How much does the job pay?" She knew she had to ask but to her ears, it sounded so shallow.

Mr. Gorgeous turned around and looked at her hard, so hard that Shasta swallowed and took a quick breath. Had she been too hasty in asking? She needed a job and should have been thankful he'd offered her one. She started to speak but Mr. Gorgeous' next words silenced her.

"The job pays $2.15 an hour plus tips. If you make it work on time every day, there's an extra ten dollars added to your pay check each month. Do you want the job?" Shasta wanted to say HELL Yeah but gave her most winning smile and replied, 'Yes'. Mr. Gorgeous smiled and turned to walk away again but this time Shasta stopped him but grabbing his arm. Later she would tell herself that grabbing him was the only way to stop him from walking away but when he turned around and looked at her, her whole insides began to tremble.

"Don't you want to know my name, where I'm from? I don't even know your name." Shasta couldn't say more. She was afraid of sounding too eager.

"My name is Thomas Edward Jr. You can call me Tommy, everyone does. Your name is..."

"Shasta, Shasta Brown. I'm from Virginia." Tommy nodded and Shasta could finally feel herself relax. She knew she couldn't just stand there and stare at him all day, so she started backing up towards the door. A few customers had come in and Tommy set menus down in front of them before heading into the kitchen. Shasta took her leave then and nearly skipped her way back to the hotel. She would be making $2.15 plus tips. That was incredible. As a store manager, she barely made $3.00 an hour and now she would be getting tips too.

Although she didn't know how long she would be working or if it was full or part time, she was excited. She knew that mostly had to do with Tommy. Tommy. She grinned. Thomas Edward Jr. sure was one amazing man and he smelled so good. Tommy was a man that she realized she definitely wanted to get to know a whole lot better.

Once she got to the hotel, Shasta sat on the bed thinking about Tommy. She wondered if he was married, had children, or was interested in a woman like her. She did consider herself a woman. She was grown now, she moved away from home, and now had a good paying job. She took a nap thinking about Tommy but once Seth came in and woke her up, her thoughts of Tommy quickly disappeared.

"How was your day sweetheart?" Seth asked waking her up. Shasta rubbed her eyes not realizing it was Seth. It took her a minute to get herself together but she smiled once Seth sat on the bed and massaged her shoulders.

"It was good." Shasta replied. "How was work?" She asked.

"Oh man it was rough, but awesome I might add. It's really hot out there too! I made a few connections and next week I will be a full time construction worker." He said proudly.

"So we should be getting an apartment soon?"

"Yes, we will. I want you to look for an apartment in the surrounding area. Hopefully we can put a deposit on an apartment next week." Seth explained. He got up, stripped his clothes off to get in the shower.

Shasta nodded, she was happy to get out of the small hotel room. She was ready to live like a real New Yorker. She figured after work she'd get the local paper and look for apartments. Just then she realized she forgot to tell Seth about her good news.

"Seth," she called out while interrupting him singing in the shower.

"Yes dear."

"I wanted to tell you something. I got good news."

"What's that?" He asked.

"I got a job at the local diner."

"Really, that is great news dear. So when do you start?"

"I start tomorrow. I go in at ten in the morning. I don't know when I'm getting off but when I do I will look in the paper for an apartment."

"You can also ask around the diner. There are hundreds of people that eat breakfast in the morning. I'm sure someone could point you in the right direction. See I told you we'd do fine up here."

"You sure did babe." Shasta grinned.

"After I get out the shower I'm going to get us something to eat. We must celebrate."

Another smile touched Shasta's face. She was glad that Seth was happy. They both would be making decent money and living the life she once only dreamed of.

Chapter 26

Shasta rushed to the diner this morning, she didn't want to be late. What she really wanted to do was to impress Tommy. It was 9:30 when she got to the diner. Tommy informed her yesterday before she left to enter in the side door. That's where she would get her apron and help Cousin Becky with the prep. She knocked on the heavy metal door and smiled as soon as Tommy opened it. It was something about his smile that made Shasta feel safe and warm inside.

"Good morning, nice to see you...thirty minutes prior to opening. That's what I like to see." He looked at his watch and gestured her to come in.

"Thanks. I noticed yesterday you guys were open before ten, is that common?"

"Oh of course, there are times when Steve and Greg come in for their morning coffee early. Then there's a couple that comes in and have breakfast. If I'm here and someone is at the door, I open it. There's no need to have someone wait when they're willing to spend their money." He laughed.

Shasta laughed right with him, she figured that was smart for business. "If I had a business I would do the same thing." she responded.

"Cousin Becky isn't here just yet. Once she gets here she will show you where to prep the food."

"Is there anything you want me to do before she gets here?" Shasta asked. She looked around the diner eager to learn the ropes. "One day I want to own a business like this."

"Can you cook?" Tommy asked.

"Kinda, but it's never too late to learn." She replied.

"That's a good spirit. Well since Becky isn't here yet, you can learn how to work the register. Ever worked something like this before?" He asked as they walked to the register.

"Yeah, they practically all work the same. I was a cashier before."

"That's cool. How'd you like that job?"

"It gave me experience. I didn't like the manager too much. She tried to get me fired."

"Why?" Tommy's concern warmed Shasta's heart.

"Uh..." she pondered for a minute. She wasn't sure if she should tell him the truth. She didn't want to get fired on her first day of work. "Well...rumor got around that my boyfriend was white. They weren't too fond of it and wanted to get me fired. So instead I ran off and end up here."

Tommy eyes widened. Shasta couldn't tell what he was thinking. "Please don't fire me." She pleaded.

He shook his head. "I wouldn't fire you. I think interracial couples are different. But you can't help who you love. Is the boy with you now, in New York?"

"Yes...yes he is."

"How long do you think that will last?"

"Excuse me?"

"You and him living in a big city. There's a lot of people in New York. Do you think your relationship will last forever?" Tommy asked in all seroiusness.

Shasta could see where this conversation was going. "I don't know, I mean he's my first relationship. I had some doubts once I moved here. It's not fair how easy he has it. He got a job immediately after we came here. If it weren't for you, I'd still be outside getting doors slammed in my face."

"I know it's not easy. Whites don't want blacks to be successful, not in this day in age anyhow." He scoffed.

"Are you upset that my boyfriend is white?" She wanted to know the truth.

"No, however I want you to be careful. You're young and I don't want anything to happen to you. If you need anything, anything at all just let me know."

"Okay."

"Now let's get back to this register." Although she told Tommy she knew how to work it, he showed her what he expected. Shasta was a fast learner and by the time Cousin Becky came in, she already knew how to cash people out. A few customers came and went. Cousin Becky was running late, for at least an hour Tommy and Shasta was running the diner together. She liked the feeling and knew she was right at home.

Cousin Becky came in shortly after 11 and Shasta worked beside her until one o'clock. Tommy came in and told her to take a ten minute break and Shasta was grateful. Cousin Becky was nice but it was stifling hot in the kitchen. She took a seat at the counter and wiped her brow. She remembered Tommy told her the fountain drinks were free but to put them in the white foam cups with the tan lids. She filled her cup up with orange soda and sat down for a spell. Stevie Wonder's latest song played in the background and she softly tapped her foot to the beat. The door chimed and she watched as a young, sharply dressed woman in red came in and sat down at a table near the door.

Tommy was in the kitchen and Shasta was considering coming off her break to take her drink order when Tommy came out of the kitchen. The lady in red waved Tommy over to her and Tommy looked at Shasta briefly before continuing to the woman's table. As soon as Tommy was close enough, the woman pulled him close to her and whispered in his ear. Tommy straightened himself and backed away from the table. To Shasta he looked uncomfortable and she felt an instant dislike for the woman in red. Just who was she and what did she mean if anything to Tommy? She knew if anyone knew it was Cousin Becky. She quickly finished her drink and made her way back to the kitchen, hoping cousin Becky had the answers that she sought.

****

Cousin Becky was stirring fresh collard greens in the huge pot when Shasta walked into the kitchen. Shasta was hungry but didn't have any money and wasn't a beggar. Tommy didn't talk to her about what she could eat or not eat or what was the pricing for employees, so Shasta decided that she wouldn't eat until she had money. She hoped that now that she was back in the kitchen, her stomach wouldn't betray her.

"You're back early. Why is that?" Cousin Becky asked and Shasta quickly came up with an appropriate answer. At least she hoped it was.

"Some people started to come in and it seemed like we might get a little rush so I came back here to help." Shasta paused for effect. She wanted to ask about that woman without seeming nosy so she silently counted to ten and went into her spiel.

"I was actually going to take a few drink orders but suddenly this woman in all red came in. She was dressed real sharp too. Red high heels, red bellbottom jumpsuit with silver sequins at the hem,big gold sunglasses, red designer purse and..."

"Did she have a mole above her upper lip?" Cousin Becky asked and Shasta nodded.

"Oh, boy. That's Veronica Boykin. She's Tommy's ex fiance. If she's here, that spells trouble. She's a gold digger. Excuse me dear." Cousin Becky left the kitchen and walked out toward the table by the door. Shasta couldn't hear her but she had taken Tommy away from the table and they were at the counter talking softly. Tommy looked up and caught Shasta staring at them and Shasta ducked back into the kitchen. She briefly wondered if Cousin Becky was telling Tommy that she saw him with Veronica and that was why she had come out of the kitchen to talk to him. She really had no idea but she was glad that Tommy was away from that she devil. She didn't deserve a good man like Tommy and Shasta wasn't going to let her sink her claws into him this time.

A few minutes later, Cousin Becky came back into the kitchen and informed Shasta that Tommy wanted to see her out front. Shasta wasn't really worried but frowned when she pushed through the door and saw that Veronica was still there. She no longer sat at the table but she was on the pay phone and was practically glaring her way. Shasta rolled her eyes and walked over to the counter. Tommy was handing a man his change and after the man walked away, he asked Shasta to take a seat.

"Why don't you shadow Antoinette for the rest of the day? She'll be here in about half an hour and will stay until we close. You've been doing well with the drink orders and cashing out the orders. You'll be a big help to her when she arrives." Tommy said and walked from around the counter.

"I thought I was shadowing you...I mean I thought you would be showing me the ropes for the rest of the day." Shasta was disappointed. She couldn't help but feel like Tommy was distancing himself because of Veronica.

"And I will but right now, I have some things to take care of. I'll be back long before we close. I've cashed out all the customers. The tips are yours. Any problems get Becky. I won't be long." Tommy touched her shoulder and walked out of the diner. A scant moment later, so did Veronica. Shasta sighed.

She knew she had a man at home but something about Tommy made her forget all about Seth. When she was around him, she felt at home. She felt like she belonged. She didn't want that feeling to end. She closed her eyes and prayed Tommy was telling Veronica to kiss him where the sun didn't shine. Her heart literally beamed at the thought and somehow, she knew everything would be alright.

Chapter 27

It had been a few weeks and finally Seth and Shasta settled into their new apartment. It wasn't lavish and a lot needed to be done. Thankfully it came with a small couch that pulled out into a bed. It was a small apartment. Less than 800 square ft. It was nothing like back home but it was affordable. Seth had to put the small place in his name because the landlord would not rent to Shasta and him. Shasta was a bit upset but they had a place and that was most important. At least that's what Seth kept telling her.

The place had exposed brick throughout, and there was a small bed with a dresser in the bedroom. Shasta bought towels and washcloths. Seth bought food and for a while things appeared to be perfect. Seth went to work and came home and Shasta brought dinner from the diner.

Tommy appeared in her thoughts at times but not as often as she thought it would. Veronica continued to visit the diner, distracting Tommy. The more Veronica came to the diner the more Tommy appeared distant. Cousin Becky said Veronica must want something otherwise she wouldn't be at the diner.

Tonight Shasta and Seth were having pot roast, green beans, mash potatoes and gravy. Cousin Becky had boxed up her food. She became Shasta's best friend.

They talked a lot while prepping and Shasta found out Cousin Becky had a son and husband. She was living her happily ever after and Shasta wanted the same thing. She wasn't too happy about Seth being in Shasta's life but she believed it was just a phase. She didn't believe in interracial relationships, but she didn't treat Shasta any less. "You'll grow out of it and find a strong black man." Is what she'd usually say.

Shasta walked into the dim apartment and set the table. She knew Seth would be in shortly and she wanted to have a nice dinner. She changed into something a little more comfortable and lit the candles. And shortly after just as she suspected Seth walked in the door.

"Hey sweetheart." Seth said walking into their small bedroom.

"Hey, how was work?"

"Good, dinner's ready?"

"Yes as always. Go ahead and wash your hands and let's eat." She gestured him to the kitchen to wash his hands.

"Wow, this looks good. You know I can get use to eating this diner food. I never had food like this back home. My folks didn't know how to make pot roast and my mom's green beans were always hard and unflavored."

Shasta wanted to laugh but she knew that would be rude. "Yeah," was all she was able to say.

"You know I really enjoy being in New York. I have a few co-workers that want to go out with tonight and grab a beer. Is it okay if I leave after dinner?" He asked.

Shasta was baffled. She thought they were going to watch movies like they usually do. "Uhh..."

"Please sweetheart, I really never got the chance to hang out in this beautiful city."

"Well I haven't either."

"I will take you out...promise. As soon as I see what's out there. I don't want you out yet because I don't know where it's really safe."

"That's true. Well have a fun time and be careful." She warned.

"I will." Seth quickly finished his dinner. Got dressed and headed out. Shasta was left home alone and that's when she started thinking about Cousin Becky. She wondered if Cousin Becky's husband went out all the time. She bundled herself on the sofa with her blanket and watched the color picture on the television screen. Seth got a television from his boss. It appeared he was getting a lot of things since he started with that company. It was hard for Shasta to continue to be happy for him. A part of her was starting to get jealous.

He seemed to be living the good life while Shasta felt like a secret. It wasn't like back home where they had to hide. She felt Seth was only saying that to her because he was embarrassed of her. She'd let it go this time, but the next time he went out he would have to take her or else.

****

Seth tried to creep through the door but Shasta was wide awake.

"It's after 3:00am, why are you creeping in the house?" She sat on the sofa in the dark with her arms folded across her chest.

"I...I was out with the fellas." Seth replied. Shasta couldn't see him but from the slur of his words she knew he was drunk.

"So this is what you do, go out and get drunk?" She asked. She dared not raise her voice, what was done was done.

"I know...I know...one drink lead to another and then another and all of a sudden I was stumbling out the bar. My friend Ken told me I could stay over but I knew I had to get home to you."

"Seth this can't happen anymore, it's not fair that you stay out this late. I thought something happened to you..."

Seth hiccupped, causing Shasta to roll her eyes, she got up and walked him to their bedroom. She turned the light on so they both could see. She then helped him with his clothes and put him in the bed.

"Thank you, thank you so much. I had an...an amazing time. Next time I go out, you're going with me...promise." He mumbled.

Shasta shook her head and grinned. She couldn't help but giggle inside due to Seth's intoxication. She folded his shirt and pants. As she placed them on the chair her smile quickly turned into a frown. She noticed red lipstick on his collar, she looked at Seth who was sound asleep. She took another look and noticed the same lipstick print on the side of his ear. She shook Seth and got on top of him demanding answers.

"Who did you kiss...who did you kiss!" She yelled.

"What are you talking about? I didn't do anything." He said half asleep.

"Why is there lipstick on your collar? Tell me why!" This time she wasn't going to talk softly, she didn't care who listened.

"Shasta I danced with a girl, a guy pushed her and she bumped into me. It was no big deal, I don't want anyone but you...trust me on that. I wouldn't bring us all this way just to cheat on you." He replied. He looked Shasta dead in the eyes and she thought she saw the truth. She hit him with the pillow and went in the living room. There was no way she was going to sleep with him tonight. She wasn't in the mood, besides she still had to get up in the morning.

Chapter 28

"I don't know, but you know how I feel. I don't like em. I don't trust any white men, and truthfully you can't trust white women either. They out here wanting our men and just as whorish as all hell." Cousin Becky rolled the dough fine and flat to make her butter ball croissants.

"I don't know, I think he's telling the truth. I'll see what happens in the next couple of days."

"Now be careful. You and Tommy.... I just don't know when ya'll gonna learn. They say you're a fool when you're young. Don't just listen to what Seth say watch what he do." She warned.

"I know and I will...believe me. I started saving up some money anyways. Just in case he tries to leave me out on a limb. Things have been a little fishy; he keeps all the bills away from me. Every first of the month he tells me he got the rent. At first it was cute but now, I think he's hiding something."

"Do you think he really be at work?" Cousin Becky asked.

"Yeah, he leaves before me."

"And when does he come home?"

"After me."

"That's what I was afraid you were going to say."

"What are you implying Becky?" Shasta asked, she needed answers.

"Oh I don't know, but men are slick. I haven't met Seth and I probably never will. I don't want you stuck. I don't want you so deep in love that when things go wrong with you and Seth it's hard for you to see a way out."

Shasta was confused about what Cousin Becky meant. She figured she was just rambling. Tommy warned Shasta about that. Cousin Becky would rant on and on not allowing anyone to get a word in. Sometimes it made sense and other times not quite. Shasta nodded out of respect. She didn't want to argue. Her attention soon was taken away when Tommy came in the back.

"Shasta I need you out front, we're getting slammed."

Saved by Tommy, she immediately followed him. She didn't bother to turn around to see if Cousin Becky needed her to stay. Shasta grabbed the apron from around her neck and sat it on the counter before heading out front.

Shasta cashed out the four customers who were waiting out front at the counter. She warmed them with her smile as they were a bit antsy from waiting. "How was your food?" she asked a few customers, making small talk.

"It was delicious! Boy do I have to come again." The one customer responded.

"Good, I'm glad. Now you make sure you come back okay." Shasta gave another one of her irresisible smiles and the guy couldn't help but blush.

"I sure will." The old man walked out the diner happier than when he came in.

"Thank you for your patience. Sometimes we get a slew of customers all at once and at the moment we are understaffed." Tommy explained to a few customers.

Shasta nodded as she finished cashing the customers out. She then pulled Tommy to the side. "May I go back now?" She asked. She didn't want any of the waitresses thinking there was something between her and Tommy.

"I kinda wanted you up here in the front for a bit. We haven't talked for the last couple of days. What's going on with my friend?" He playfully tapped her on the shoulder. Shasta glanced at the waitresses who went back to waiting on tables. They appeared to be really busy, maybe they weren't paying them any attention.

"Nothing. You and Miss Lady in Red were spending so much time together, you forgot I was working here." Tommy was shocked at the response Shasta gave, he never thought someone so sweet would display such attitude.

"Well…"

"Well what, you can be honest. All of the customers are eating, nobody is paying us any attention. Cousin Becky is in the back working her butt off. It's just you and me…go ahead you can be honest."

"She was my ex fiancé."

"Was…as in …"

"She was, there's no more us. She comes every once and a while. The downfall is that she was my first love. It's hard not help her when she's in need."

Shasta raised her eyebrows. "You think it's wise to be so vulnerable? What did she want if you don't mind me asking?"

"Money as usual," he scoffed. "She needed help with rent. Her father is going through something and she used all her money for his medical bills."

"Oh I see, so when she calls, you come running?" Shasta knew her question was a low blow but she didn't have any remorse.

"Gee why so upset. I didn't think you cared."

"Well I don't," Shasta walked to the back of the room where nobody could see them. Her intentions were to get away from Tommy but he followed her. "Look what we and Miss Lady in Red...I mean Veronica have is nothing. She needed help and I gave it to her. You have a boyfriend." He leaned over to her, "A white one at that! You have no room for throwing bricks."

"You started flirting with me first, implying that you're interest in me." Shasta snapped back.

"Why do you think I like you?" Tommy asked.

"Because you hired me," Shasta put her hands on her hips and moved her head from side to side. She had confidence and Tommy witnessed it.

Tommy moved closer to her. Shasta immediately stepped back. He grabbed her hand and caressed it. "I do like you Shasta, I like you a lot."

Shasta got butterflies in her stomach. Tommy's fresh scent made Shasta melt. Putting him on the table and ripping his clothes off were the thoughts going through her head. She held her composure and moved her hand. "I know you do." She said and walked off toward the door outside. Tommy called out to her. "I'm going on my break." She grinned right before opening the door to let herself out. She made sure she didn't turn around to see the expression on Tommy's face.

****

Shasta finished the rest of her shift without any issues. The butterflies would not go away however and each time Tommy looked her way, she thought about the way she walked off. What if she never did that? She caught him staring at her a few times but Veronica came back and this time she wore a metallic gold halter jumpsuit. Shasta had to hand it to her, she did look sensational although she had a bad vibe about that girl. Becky kinda gave her the 411 about Veronica and Tommy.

Thanks to Becky, Shasta found out Veronica and Tommy met about eight years ago. Long before Tommy bought *Sweet Daddy's Restaurant*; later named *Sweet Daddy Tommy's Soul Food Restaurant.* When Tommy met Veronica he was nineteen years old. Had been living in New York for nearly seven years, and was a good boy. Veronica's looks and fast talking swept him off his feet. As he mentioned before, she was his first love. He wanted to give her everything. He worked three jobs to buy her the finer things she craved. Thing was, she didn't just crave Tommy. She'd gotten accustomed to a specific lifestyle and wanted more. Tommy wanted to please her. He needed to please her.

He was warned about Veronica more than once from friends. He didn't see anything wrong with her and focused on working and making a better living for himself. Growing up his relatives talked about him getting out of the ghetto and he listened to all the stories of the past and decided at a young age he would work was his way out of the ghetto.

He wanted to be someone like the father he never got to know who died way too young. He admired his older relatives and Becky was his favorite cousin. She was fifteen years older than Tommy but had a wealth of knowledge and could COOK! That's where Tommy got his idea to open up *Sweet Daddy Tommy's Soul Food Restaurant*, A.K.A the corner diner. The diner had been open for four years now but it was Tommy's pride and joy. Everything on the menu Tommy came up with. All Becky had to do was cook the food. Antoinette, Dawn and Shawna were the waitresses. Tommy kept it a family restaurant with the exception of Shasta. She was the only exception. Shasta sighed. She'd been given a chance and at a young age, she realized second chances didn't come easy.

She was thankful for the job at the diner and for Tommy. His name alone sent the butterflies fluttering in her stomach. She knew she shouldn't feel this way, couldn't feel this way but she did. She just had to figure out what she should do about it.

****

Her thoughts continued to linger as she sat alone on the couch waiting for Seth to walk in. She twiddled her fingers for a few minutes and decided to put the food she from the diner into the oven. It was baked chicken and dressing. She had enough macaroni and cheese for three or four people and corn bread muffins. Becky gave her some banana pudding too and she set it in a glass bowl in the refrigerator. She sat back down on the couch and before long, she was fast asleep.

It was after eight when Shasta woke up. She peered at the clock on the wall. What the HELL!! Where in the hell was Seth! Shasta got up from the couch and paced back and forth. Seth should have been home by now. Truthfully, he should have been home two hours ago. She looked out the window and saw no sign of him. His moped wasn't out front. She was pissed beyond words.

She went into the kitchen and took the food out of the oven. The oven was on warm and the food was piping hot. She looked at the food and no longer had an appetite. She tried not to, but she began to cry. Why was Seth doing this? She knew what was going on and she could feel her heart break in two. He promised her that he'd protect her, and he wouldn't cheat on her but in her heart of hearts, she knew that was exactly what was going on.

It was after ten when Seth finally brought his ass home. Shasta was in bed, feigning sleep and heard him in the kitchen. *Oh no he wasn't in there fixing him some food!* She should have thrown the food out if she knew what was good for her. She let out a frustrated sigh and was about to get up, head into the kitchen and confront him but something held her back. She laid back down and silently counted to ten. Seth slithered his way into the bathroom and came out a few minutes later and slid between the sheets. He reached over and grabbed Shasta arm and drew her close, as if she wouldn't know he'd just gotten in. Still Shasta said nothing.

She smelled the mint on his breath and knew he had just used some mouthwash in the bathroom. She closed her eyes just to open them again. She sniffed. She smelled lavender and a hint of rosemary. Wow. She closed her eyes again and held the tears at bay. She would not cry with him in her presence and she most definitely would not shed any tears for him tonight.

Chapter 29

Shasta was up early the next morning. Who was she kidding, she never went to sleep. Around 10:30, she eased out of the bed and sat on the couch. She had to think. She'd been working nearly two months for Tommy and had a little money saved up but not much. Seth paid the bills but a few days ago had asked her to get the groceries and house essentials since he wouldn't get paid until next week. Shasta hadn't minded then but she could really use that $75 now.

Seth was still asleep looking as if he had no worries. Only Seth knew what he was doing with his idle time. And why all of a sudden was it he couldn't pay for groceries and household essentials? He did before. She thought of ways to confront him all night but knew he'd deny it. She almost felt like she had to catch him red handed but would she ever? They truthfully didn't run in the same circles. Already Seth had several dock guys as friends and the only people in New York she could call friend was Becky, Antoinette, Shawna and of course Tommy. Tommy was much more to her than a friend. She sighed again and heard the shower. Seth was awake.

Shasta paced the living room floor. She didn't want to hear the pack of lies Seth was going to feed her. She slowly counted to twenty and went down the hall. She heard the shower stop. She went into the bedroom and waited. Seth had to come back in there to finish getting ready. It was shortly before eight. As it turned out, Seth dressed in the bathroom and Shasta watched as he flew past the bedroom and into the living room. Shasta stood and walked out into the living room. Seth had his head in the refrigerator and came out with a bagel and an orange in his hand. When he saw Shasta he looked startled at first but then he pasted on a dazzling smile.

"Hey, sweetheart. I see you're up. You want a bagel or something. I don't see any cream cheese but there's some grape jelly in there and...."

"Seth where were you last night? I know you didn't get in from your 9-5 job until after ten o'clock and before you try to pretend like you didn't I was up. Need I remind you that you have to pass my side of the bed to get into the bathroom. Need I say more?" Shasta felt steam coming out of her ears and felt the sting of tears threatening to fall yet she held them back.

"I know I was out late. I'm sorry but I just couldn't tell you what I'd done." Seth didn't say anymore and Shasta's mind was already going there so she turned from him and closed her eyes. She wasn't prepared for this, not any of it. Seth moved in front of her and lifted up his shirt. It was a tattoo with the initials SB with a heart around it and an arrow through it. Shasta didn't know what to say. She was ready to count Seth out, then this.

"I didn't know if you liked tats or not but I had to get it. It's you babe. Shasta Brown, my girl. I hope you like it. I really gotta get to work babe. I don't want to be late. See you tonight." Seth gave her a quick peck on the cheek and walked out the door. Shasta stood there and watched the closed door long after Seth had gone.

Shasta arrived to work just after 9:30. She saw Tommy's clean black Cadillac parked up front. She was so confused. Seth's tattoo with her initials should have made her happy but she still felt at a loss. Something just didn't ring true to her. She didn't know what to do.

She sat down at the counter and hung her head to think and when she lifted her head, Tommy stood before her. He sat down close enough that she smelled his breath. He smelled like peppermint. He was watching her and suddenly stood up.

"You look like hell. You go out and party all night or what?"

"It's the *what* that has me feeling like hell." Shasta stood up and looked Tommy dead in the eye. Tommy moved closer and was about to say something. Shasta could feel it but suddenly, they were getting a rush. About ten people came into the diner all at once and then several more filed in. Antoinette, Shawna and Dawn came out of the kitchen to start taking orders and Shasta ran into the kitchen to help Becky.

Of course Tommy handled it like a pro and by 11:00, everyone was fed and the diner was filled with happy customers. Shasta caught Tommy's eye and watched as he walked off toward the storage room. Shasta didn't know why but she followed him. When she got inside the room, Tommy was bent over a cart carrying vegetable oil, flour and sugar and other spices. He found what he sought and when he rose , Shasta was barely three feet from him.

Tommy smiled and handed Shasta the all spice for the sweet potato pies. Shasta took it but stood still, not moving a muscle. Tommy looked at her questioningly and took a step forward.

"That's for Becky. She wanted to get started on the pies before noon. She says there's only a few in the refrigerator that's left." Shasta nodded but still didn't move. Tommy took another step and Shasta finally got the courage to speak.

"You started to say something to me earlier before we got slammed. What was it?" Shasta asked and watched as Tommy shook his head.

"It was nothing. You should get that to Becky before she comes looking for it." Tommy walked past Shasta but she grabbed his hand, pulling him back.

"I don't believe you. You wanted to say something. I know you did. What was it? Was it about work? Was it about me or..."

"Just let it go Shasta."

"What if I don't want to? What if I don't want to let it go? What then?"

"Look, you have a boyfriend remember, a very white boyfriend at that. You were right, I shouldn't have flirted with you. It seems you have enough complications right now and Lord knows I have my own. Let's just forget about yesterday. It will be best for both of us." Tommy said but Shasta wasn't hearing any of that. She couldn't forget and Lord knows how hard she tried. Tommy was unforgettable. Everything about him was, and she was learning that the hard way.

"My relationship right now is complicated..."

"What did you expect?" Tommy replied cutting her off. "Did you think it would be easy? Your 'relationship' is *tainted.* It's what they call Tainted Love. I should know. I was in a tainted relationship. It was doomed from the start. V always had an ulterior motive and she never took no for an answer. I granted her every whim. I aimed to please and always came up short. No matter what I did, she wanted more. No matter how much I spent, it was never enough. The men, the clothes, the shoes, the cars, V's name in lights...you know she had me do that for her once. One fourth of July she demanded it of me. I did it too. I wanted to make her happy. Little did I know I never would, never could because I was never enough!" Shasta listened on and touched Tommy's cheek. She didn't know who moved first but soon she stood just inches away from him.

She thought Tommy was done speaking when he suddenly began talking again. "You may think you love him but you don't. You're probably like me, just in love with love for the sake of wanting it so badly. You want to feel cherished. You want to feel secure and safe. You want to be in love like everyone else. That was me. I'd see couples holding hands and want to be them. I'd see a man caress his woman's cheek and want the same. But now I know... it took me a while to figure it out but now I know."

"What do you know?" Shasta asked in a whisper.

"I know that love clouds all thinking. I know love has no reasoning and I know love is not for me."

"Don't say that! Love *is* for you! Love is for everybody. There's someone out there for each of us to love..."

"And have you met your true love huh, Shasta? Is this boy your love match? Does he treat you like an equal? Does he keep all his promises and never lie to you? Does he put you first? Does he make you feel welcomed around HIS people or are you hiding in the shadows? Does he introduce you to all his friends and tell them that you're his and he's yours? Does he? If he isn't then there's a problem, because if you were my woman I'd shout it from the highest rooftop. I'd show you around town and let everyone know we were one. There would be NO DOUBT in anyone's mind, least of all yours. There would be no doubt..." Tommy leaned in close and just as he was about to kiss her, Becky opened the storage door.

Chapter 30

"Well I'll be damn. I was wondering what was taking so long?" Cousin Becky clearly ignored what she just witnessed. "I got pies to make, hand me those things so I can get back to work." She snatched the spices off of Shasta. "Don't let me stop you," she gave a sly smile as she headed out the storage room.

"I think that was our cue to get out of here." Tommy brushed past Shasta.

She wasn't ready to be out of his presence. She wanted him to stand there and tell her how he felt about her. "Would you be happier with me?" The bold question stopped Tommy in his tracks.

He turned around and gave Shasta a dumb look. "Of course I would be. However no matter how we think we feel," he pointed to her and himself. "We have issues outside of this would be fling. It's not fair that we both have someone we *think* we care about. I think things need to be straight before proceeding any further. Honestly a part of me doesn't care for V, but there's still that small part that does."

"I understand. I don't want to be in competition nor do I want you to be. I care about you." She replied softly. "I think about you nonstop each day. I only wish we'd take our past and throw them over the Brooklyn Bridge."

Tommy couldn't help but chuckle. "Right but life isn't always that simple." He walked out the room before she could say another word.

She leaned against one of the cabinets and slid to the floor. She covered her head with her arms. She wanted to scream but that wasn't a good idea. A few customers were still out there and she didn't want anyone to think something was wrong. She really didn't want anyone in her business. However she knew she could talk to Cousin Becky. She knew the way to get through to Tommy was through her.

Shasta quickly got off the floor and headed to the kitchen. The waitresses were out front counting their money and changing out the register. She knew this was the perfect time to talk to Cousin Becky without any interruptions.

Cousin Becky gave her another one of her sly smiles as soon as she entered the room. "It was only a matter of time," she replied.

"What do you mean?" Shasta returned the sly smile back at Cousin Becky.

"You know what I mean. It's obvious you two got something going on. I knew he cared for you the moment you walked into the diner. He thought about you all day and hoped you come back and luckily you did."

"Yeah." Shasta sighed. "Looks like the two of us are going to only *want* each other. He has feelings for Veronica and my situation ain't squeaky clean."

"I understand but time will tell. I must admit Veronica put a tamper on that boy's heart. My soul cringes every time her scent hits the back of this kitchen. I get sick and tired of her coming in and out of his life. It's downright pitiful." She rolled the dough out to make the crust for the pie. Shasta sat on a stool and day dreamed of them being together one day.

"So..." Cousin Becky said, snapping her out of her thoughts.

"So?"

"Answer the question."

"What question?"

"What's going on with you and Seth? I mean you know I don't like the boy but what's going on now?"

Shasta sighed. She really didn't want to hear Cousin Becky's opinion on Seth, but she figured she walked right into that. "He comes home later every night."

"Hmm."

"He came home after 10pm last night. I confronted him on it and he showed me what he'd been doing."

"What's that?" Cousin Becky put her hands on her hip. She had the rolling pin in her hand as if she was going to hit someone upside the head with it.

"A tattoo. He wasn't sure if that was something I was into but he surely was."

"What's the tattoo of?"

"My initials." Shasta didn't dare look at Cousin Becky for her reaction.

"Say what!" She covered her mouth. "I wonder what made him get that."

"I don't know, I wonder too."

"Girl...watch out for him. I don't know what's going on in his brain but he clearly is loving him some Shasta Brown. I didn't think they were all that good in the bed no way."

Shasta giggled, only Cousin Becky would say something crazy like that. "I don't know what's going on but I don't think that's an excuse for him to come in that late. I don't think tattoo's take an eternity to complete."

"It depends on where he went, was it nice at least?"

"It sure was, and it was huge. Right on his chest, he smiled when he showed it to me too." Shasta raised her eyebrows.

"Hmm, sounds like you and Tommy rocking in the same boat. Veronica doesn't have a tattoo of Tommy's initials but he sure as hell has her tattooed on his heart. He can't seem to let that girl go, whether it was a life or death situation."

"I know and that's want I came to talk to you about. How do I get his attention? How do I confess that I care for him?"

"Well first you gotta get rid of your vanilla cream pie before you go dippin' into that creamy chocolate." Cousin Becky had some crazy sayings. "Then...maybe we can figure something out."

Shasta had some thinking to do. She didn't know what she was going to do, but she had to make a move.

Chapter 31

Shasta went home with Tommy on her mind. She soon noticed a woman and her girls walking up the street. She reminisced about her mother and sister. She wondered if they were okay and if they even cared she'd been gone for over three months.

She missed talking to her sister. She wanted to go home and visit but that wasn't an option. People back home wanted her to fail and she wasn't going to give them reason to laugh at her. She wondered if Seth missed his family. He was so closed to them, his sacrifice made her realize how sweet he was. If it wasn't for him they would still be at that cabin or hiding out somewhere in Virginia trying to see each other. She wondered if she was in Virginia at this moment, would they even still be together.

Tommy had a point to what he said to her earlier at the diner. Seth never took her out, his promises soon faded away and every time he made a new one she ignored him. She knew in due time she'd figure out what to do with him. She felt Seth gave her a reason to live and conquer her dreams, but was he just a seasonal boyfriend? Was it time for her to move on and be happy with the few memories they did have? She opened the door, sat down on the couch and sighed. Tommy was right, her love was tainted.

To her surprise Seth was home. He was in the bedroom and startled her when he walked over to where she sat on the couch. She didn't expect him to be home since he rarely was in on time.

"Hey sweetheart, how are you feeling?" He sat on the couch with her, took her shoes off and rubbed her feet."

"Tired, dead tired work was crazy and we had multiple rushes."

"How long do you think you'll be working at that diner?"

"I don't know why, you thinking of relocating?"

"No, not necessarily. I was just making small talk."

"How was work for you?" She asked.

"It was good, but I came home sick."He sighed. "I wasn't feeling good and the boss told me to go home. I've been drinking tea and eating the left over soup in the refrigerator . We actually just ran out. I want to go out to the store and get some more."

"I'll go since you're sick." She replied.

"No sweetheart that's alright. I need to get some fresh air. I've been cooped up in this apartment for way too long." He put his jacket on and headed out the door. Shasta didn't bother to stop him. The moment he closed the door she thought about the lady walking down the street with her two daughters.

The thought of the woman made her decide to write a letter to her sister. She needed to let out her feelings. She truly missed them but she didn't want to take the risk of them tracking where she lived. The best way to write the letter was sending it without a return address. She took a pen and paper bunched up on the couch and gathered her thoughts.

Hey sis,

All is well. I miss you and Ma so much, but as you know I can't come home. How are things, how is Ma? Tell her I'm okay but please don't share this letter with her. I wanted to let you know I'm working and making a little bit of money. I'm still with Seth and things are looking okay. I have a small apartment, really small but the New York life is great. I'm meeting new people. Most of all my boss is black along with the staff. It's a family business! He owns his own diner and gave me a shot. Isn't that wonderful?

Any who I don't want to bore you. I miss you very, very much. Maybe one day in the future I can come visit. Right now is just way too soon.

Love you,

Shasta

She imprinted her cherry lips on the letter. She put the address on the envelop but left no return address. She'd drop it in the mail box tomorrow morning on her way to work. She felt good about writing that letter. She knew Cassie would be relieved. She had to let someone out there know she was still okay.

Shasta took a shower and got in the bed. She wasn't in the mood to eat, thoughts took over her hunger. She closed her eyes and went to sleep, preparing for another day at the diner.

****

When Shasta woke up from her brief nap, Seth was still gone. It was after seven and she was hungry. She realized she hadn't eaten anything all day but her mind was so consumed with thoughts of Tommy. She felt a headache coming on and went into the bathroom to look for some Tylenol. Not finding any, she realized she had some in her purse. She opened the dresser drawer to grab her purse, moving a pair of Seth's work pants to the side. That's when she saw a piece of paper sticking out of Seth's pants.

She took the piece of paper out of his pants and unfolded it. The paper was written in a female's handwriting and the handwriting looked vaguely familiar. Shasta shook her head. That just didn't make sense. The note read, *"Can't wait to see you later. Had* a *blast last night, can't believe we got matching tattoos!" Shannon B.*

Shasta nearly threw up. Who the *hell* was Shannon B? She had to be the girl Seth danced with at the party, who left her lipstick on his collar and earlobe. Shasta wanted to scream. She did scream. Why was this happening to her?

An hour after Shasta discovered the piece of paper in Seth's pants pocket she heard keys jiggle at the door. She finally sat down on the bed. Fresh tears rolled down her cheeks. She heard Seth in the living room. Was he on the phone? Did he call Shannon? Shasta got up off the bed to walk out the bedroom just as Seth entered it.

"I found what I was looking for after the third grocery store. Can you believe that? It's a mad house out there." Seth walked past Shasta into the bedroom. He didn't even notice her tear stained face.

"You're a damn liar! You are and today ends your trail of lies! What the hell is this and who the fuck is Shannon?" Shasta threw the piece of paper and it landed at Seth's feet. Seth looked surprised at first but recovered quickly.

"What's this? Come on baby. It's nothing. It's just a piece of paper I picked up off the floor the other night when I went dancing. I think it belongs to one of the guys I was out with. He must've dropped it on the floor and I picked it up..."

"Stop it! Stop it! You're lying! I know it and you know it. I'm not gonna ask again. Who the hell is Shannon? Is that the girl whose lipstick was on your shirt collar?"

"Shasta look, I don't know what you're talking about. I picked up the paper and put it in my pocket. I was drunk remember. I was out of it and..."

"Oh my God SB...Shannon B! The tattoo wasn't of my name at all but Shannon's. Oh, my frickin' God! You dirty bastard!" Shasta screamed, no longer caring who heard her. Seth walked toward her, trying to calm her down.

"Shasta, I was going to tell you. Really I was but there was never any time..."

"You lying son of a bitch! You *promised* you wouldn't do this to me!" Shasta shrieked. "You were running this game in Virginia too, weren't you?" Shasta really didn't expect an answer. Not the truth anyway.

"Baby, no. It just happened. I mean it wasn't planned but when Emily invited me here to work for her father, things started moving so fast and..."

"Emily...Emily ...Berkely? From the discount store in Virginia..." Shasta trailed off and had to shallow the bile that was threatening to surface. She remembered Emily saying her father lived in New York

City and was a foreman at the docks. She also remembered that Emily had planned to visit her father for a long time. Apparently she seized that opportunity and at Shasta's expense nonetheless.

Seth watched as Shasta connected the dots and reached out to touch her but Shasta slapped his hand away.

"You know what I went through with Emily and Ms. Peters. You know how they both treated me but you chose *Emily* to cheat on me with? You are not the man I thought you were. You're as a big a monster as they ever were."

"It wasn't like that. She apologized about how she acted at the store. She was really sorry. She was so sorry that when she said she was moving to New York, she promised me a job with her Dad if I ever came out here. She kept her end of the bargain too..."

"You came here intentionally then? You made it seem like it was our only choice to come here. We'll have a fresh start you said, but you were bringing baggage with you! It all makes sense now. And to think I was jealous of how easy you seemed to have it, never knowing you were playing me like a fiddle all along." It dawned on her then. The thing with Neil and Laquenta didn't seem so random now.

"That's not true. I care about you. I've been faithful to you. I just got caught up in the moment when I got here. I've never felt so free before and alive. I wanted to introduce you to my new friends but I just never got the chance..."

"I can't believe a word that comes out of your mouth. You're a thief, a liar and a cheat and you will never touch me again!"

"Shasta, baby I don't love Emily...Shannon. She just helped me out a lot. She helped me get a job and this great place and...."

"So everything's out the bag now. The TV must've come from Emily too. The tattoo, I guess was all on her too. She had a gun to your head, huh? Ugh! I've heard about all I can take from you." Shasta tossed items from the dresser drawer onto the bed. She grabbed her small bag from underneath the bed and threw her underwear, bras, t-shirts and jeans into the bag. She ran into the bathroom and tossed all her feminine items and toiletries into the bag. She only had one pair of shoes and she was wearing them. She was glad they were tennis shoes because all she wanted to do was use them to run as fast as she could and never return.

Chapter 32

Shasta heard Seth outside the bathroom door trying to make his way in. Shasta sunk to the floor and cried uncontrollably. Why did this happen to her? All she wanted was to be loved. Why did it have to be so hard to find?

Seth was speaking to her from outside the bathroom door but she had drowned his words out. She looked at the window and realized it was just low enough for her to reach. She could hear Seth carrying on outside the door and she hoped he continued to beg and plead for her to let him in.

She carefully opened the window and hoped the outside noise was not coming in. She knew she had to do something quick because Seth had plans to knock the door down or pick it with a knife. She couldn't risk it. Once the window was open to the height she wanted, she dared to look down. Their apartment was on the third floor, she wasn't up too high but it was high enough.

She tossed her bag outside the window and watched it land. Seth's voice was getting louder and louder and Shasta knew it wouldn't be long before he was inside that bathroom. She closed her eyes, climbed out onto the ledge and jumped.

****

Tommy pulled up to the diner and parked his Cadillac. As he was walking up to the door, he saw something pink out the corner of his eye. He realized it was something or someone bundled up just a few feet from the diner. As he got closer, he realized it was Shasta. He recognized her pink and white Nikes sticking out of the pink blanket. He reached down and lifted the blanket from over her head.

Shasta was startled and awoke quickly. She rubbed her eyes and passed a hand over her face. She focused her eyes and realized Tommy was standing in front of her. She rose quickly to her feet and started folding up the blanket.

"Shasta, what are you doing out here? Did you sleep here all night?" Tommy didn't wait for her to answer. He took her by the arm, grabbed her bag and walked her to the diner. He unlocked the door and ushered her inside. He turned on the lights, set her bag behind the counter in the far corner and motioned for Shasta to sit down. She did but with some reluctance. Her bottom was a little sore. She was glad she had thrown her bag out the window first because it helped break her fall.

"What happened to you? Your eyes are all swollen and you look like you jumped out of a four story window."

"Oh, no a three story one to be exact." Shasta tried laughing but Tommy stared at her until realization dawned on him.

"Shasta baby...are you okay? Are you in pain? I bet you're thirsty. Let me get some water." Tommy went behind the counter and grabbed a glass and filled it with ice, then water. Shasta smiled through her tears. He was so thoughtful. He was attending to her needs as if he known her for years. He was such a kind hearted man.

"Here's some aspirin. Antoinette always keeps a bottle under the counter. Take a few of them. I'll put on some coffee...." Tommy stopped and turned around. Something in Shasta's eyes made him sit back down.

"I left him...he was...he cheated on me with my worst enemy, at least one of them. He knew how they treated me. How they tried to get me fired and maybe even lynched but he still went there. I never want to see him again. I don't. It's so over between us." Shasta looked toward Tommy, hoping for understanding. Tommy got up and walked behind the counter. Shasta stared after him, confused.

"Did you just hear me? It's over. Seth and I are through...he's a liar and a cheat and I hate him! I'll never let him near me again, ever!"

Tommy sighed and started the coffee. Before long its rich aroma was traveling all over the diner. Shasta sat baffled, watching Tommy pour two cups of coffee, adding sugar and cream to both. What was wrong with him? Couldn't he hear dammit!

"What's wrong with you? I just told you my whole world just fell apart and you go and make coffee? I thought you liked me. You told me you liked me. Were you lying too?" Tommy narrowed his eyes, took a sip of his steaming hot brew and set the cup down. He stared at Shasta for half a second and walked from behind the counter.

"I'm not Seth. Don't confuse me with him ever. I'd never confuse *you* with Veronica." Shasta exhaled. She didn't want to fight with Tommy. She needed him now more than ever. Why couldn't he see that?

"You're mad right now. I get it. But see just days ago you practically professed your undying love for this boy to me. Right here in this very diner...."

"No, I was only reminding you about *both* of our complicated situations. Mine just ended. I guess it was finished before we even left Virginia but I failed to get the memo. Look, you told me if I were your woman, you'd shout it from the highest rooftop. Everyone and anybody would know I was yours and you were mine. Is that true? Did you really mean that?"

Shasta stood up and was inches away from Tommy's face.

"I meant every word of it but I'm not sure you're that over this guy. You got an overnight bag, but nothing else. It would be too easy to go back to him."

"Or just as easy to walk away, I can't go back. I gave up too much to be with him and he did this to me. I gave up my sister, my mother and my best friend. I've lost so much. I can't afford to lose anyone else." Shasta's eyes were swimming with tears and Tommy loving caught a few that escaped past her cheeks. He moved closer and suddenly the door chimed. In walked Veronica. Tommy sighed and moved in front of Shasta to shield her from Veronica's view.

"Go take your bag into the restroom and freshen up. We'll be opening soon." Shasta walked behind the counter to retrieve her bag. She didn't want to leave Tommy alone with Veronica. He had a weak spot for her and she didn't want to lose him before they could get started. Veronica slithered seductively closer to Tommy, knowing how to reel him in. Shasta hoped Tommy could resist a little while longer so that she could show him what real happiness looked like.

****

Shasta opened her overnight bag and brushed her teeth. She raised her head and for the first time she saw what Tommy saw. A disheveled, confused, mislead, and heartbroken young woman. Tears stingly fell down her cheeks. She reminisced on Seth and her journey to New York. She recalled the day she lost her virginity. The day he said he'd never leave her and the day she fell in love looking at the tall buildings in New York. She was so in awe of the city.

Her thoughts lingered on to the day they were at the bed and breakfast. The look on Seth's face when he shielded her from his uncle. Who was going to protect her now? Was she kidding herself thinking Tommy was the one for her? Was her emotions taking over? Momma always told her never to act on emotions. Shasta had searched for something to get mad at Seth about, unfortunately she found it sooner than expected.

After brushing her teeth she sat on the toilet. She was too afraid to go out and see what Tommy and Veronica was up to. She felt cheated, if she messed with Tommy, would he take her serious? Would he still put Veronica first? Would she be more of a mistress than a girlfriend? She knew Tommy and Veronica weren't married but you couldn't tell by the way he acted around her sometimes.

Once Shasta got enough energy, she washed her face and cleaned herself up. She put on a fresh pair of clothes and walked to the prep table. Cousin Becky settled in and chopped some onions and green peppers. She looked at Shasta and had to do a double take.

"What's wrong?" She put the knife down, wiped her hands on her apron and opened her arms.

Shasta immediately walked to Cousin Becky and cried on her shoulder. She didn't want to be so loud because they had a few customers inside the diner but she couldn't help it. She was hurt and even though she knew Seth cheated on her, she didn't really want to believe it. She didn't think after all they had been through he'd do this to her.

"It's really over," she cried out after letting Cousin Becky go. "He cheated on me. He really cheated on me and I left, I had to. I couldn't stay there...I can't stay there. It's not safe for me."

Cousin Becky instantly became empathetic toward her. "We knew the time was coming, you don't want any white boy no way. Our black men are better." She tried to make light of the situation. It caused Shasta to smile, but it didn't take the pain away.

"I have to figure out where I'm going to stay. I also need to get the rest of my things. I don't have much but the little I do have I do want." She replied.

“We will worry about that later. You can go shopping downtown and get some new clothes,” Cousin Becky assured her. “And I'll buy those for you.”

“Thank you, but where am I going to stay?”

“Good question,” Cousin Becky replied. “My place isn’t that big but you’re always welcome to stay. At least until you get yourself together.”

“I don’t know what else to do. I'm afraid to go back to the apartment.”

“Don’t go back today, go back tomorrow. Seth would expect you to come today to get your things. He probably stayed home. Don’t even go back tomorrow, wait a few days until the two of you cool down. You don’t want to walk in that place and start crying all over again.” Cousin Becky stated.

Shasta knew Cousin Becky was right. Once she gathered herself ,she’d get her clothes. She was thankful to have great people in her life.

“Now go in the bathroom and clean your face. We have a some customers that need feeding.” Cousin Becky said.

“Okay,” Shasta did as she was told. She forgot about Tommy and wanted to focus on work at this moment. She had a place to stay and reminded herself she would get her things from the apartment soon. She knew she had to be a survivor. As for her, that day started today.

Chapter 33

When Shasta left the kitchen from helping Cousin Becky with the prep, Veronica was gone. Tommy was talking to an older gentleman near the door. As if sensing her staring at them Tommy looked her way and quickly finished his conversation. The older gentleman nodded her way and walked out the diner. Tommy made a call on the phone and when he got finished, he saw Shasta sitting at one of the tables in the back. Shasta watched as he made his way toward her, the butterflies began to twist and turn and do somersaults. She was nervous. What would he say? Was he through with Veronica or had he decided to make her a permanent fixture in his life?

Tommy sat across from her and stared at her for a half a second. Shasta felt as if he were pacing his words, which made her more nervous than anything. She needed to know what he was thinking and how he felt.

"Earlier today you laid some heavy news on me. It was unexpected but not that surprising to me. I don't mean to say this to hurt your feelings. I think you are an amazing lady and deserving of both honor and respect, but I didn't feel that respect coming from him. I believe he was along for the ride, the adventure and the excitement. I think he thought he loved you but was only in love with the thought of you. There is a big difference." Shasta exhaled and waited intently for Tommy's next words. She didn't have to wait long.

"From that first day, when I saw you at the other diner, I knew there was something unique and special about you. You were eager even then, I felt it. Then you came here. I honestly didn't think I'd see you again yet suddenly you were right here in front of me. I knew then that the connection I felt was real. That's why I didn't charge you for the soda. I felt in my heart that you'd come back and you did. The job I offered you was meant to keep you close to me. Like I told you before, I don't hire outsiders ...just family, but you were different. I had hoped but didn't really know....you were attached and I..."

"You have Veronica." Shasta replied, causing Tommy to laugh. She really didn't see the comedy in it. So he was still holding out hope for her. Shasta felt suddenly sick. She thought that he liked her. He said he did but Veronica must have swayed him again. She sighed.

"I was going to say, had to take care of my problem for good. That's what I've been doing for the past hour and a half. My Uncle Titus was just here and was telling me about getting a protective order out on Veronica." Shasta's head was spinning out of control. A protective order? Wow. Wait...that meant Veronica had to have done something bad.

Tommy read her loud and clear. She wanted to know what happened and he'd tell her but first, there was something he needed to know.

"Are you sure it's really over between you and this guy? I don't want to lay everything on the line and this all turns out to be *loves' hangover.* You might start to feel remorse, go visiting merrylane, then poof, all's forgiven. That would be too much to take after all that my heart's been through...."

"I'm not going back. I can't go back and don't want to. I'm done. Are you?" Shasta asked and reached over the table to lightly stroke Tommy's hand. She instantly saw the heated desire in his eyes, causing a warm flush to go up her cheek. She knew what he wanted because she wanted the same. She and Seth had not been intimate in several weeks and she missed the closeness, the heat, and the passion. She knew Tommy had the ability to be passionate. She saw it each time she was alone with him, the heated desire and the passionate fire in his eyes. She wanted to feel that passion too.

"After you left last night, Veronica came back and started getting really lippy with Shawna. Usually she doesn't even speak to anyone but me when she comes in here but she got all in Shawna's face when she was with a customer. She demanded to know where I was...and who I was with. She grabbed Shawna and asked her where you lived." Tommy watched as realization flashed on Shasta's face.

"Apparently not just Becky or my other family members have noticed the attraction I have for you. Veronica found me in the back emptying trash and started really going crazy. She was drunk, and she started arguing with me. I called a cab and sent her on her way. I thought that was it. She later in the night decided it was a good idea to go to Shawna's apartment and defecate outside her apartment door. Then she sent a brick flying threw her downstairs window. One of the neighbors in the apartment saw her and when Shawna got home, she called and told me. I was upset and very worried for her. I called the police but they couldn't find her in their search so today I decided to take matters into my own hands.

After today, Veronica will not be able to come within fifty feet of me, this diner, or my home. I told Shawna to press charges too. That's why she isn't here now. She's never acted this way before but I won't take chances with my family's life or yours or anyone coming inside this restaurant. I told her to leave and never come back here. She may not listen but if she comes in here or is caught on the streets near this diner, she will be going to jail." Shasta almost couldn't contain her joy. There were only a few customers in the diner after the rush but Shasta leaned forward and whispered anyway.

"Where does that leave us? How do you feel about me? You already said that you like me a lot but do want to be with me? Do you want to touch me, kiss me?" Tommy sighed. He did want to touch her and kiss her and do a lot more but he still had customers in the diner. Most of the folks dining in were folks he'd known forever. A thought occurred to him. He left the table and talked to a few of the customers near the back and talked to the group of four near the front. Before long, the diner was empty. Shasta's eyes widened with fascination as she watched Tommy flip the open sign over to CLOSED. She was even more curious as he walked toward the kitchen, going inside. She inhaled deeply. She could hear Cousin Becky and Antoinette talking as they went out the back door.

When Tommy returned, he walked with a purpose up the isle to her table. Shasta was still a little in shock but felt giddy inside. The look in Tommy's eyes spoke volumes and Shasta's own eyes had glazed over with desire. She'd been attracted to this sexy man practically from the moment she walked in his restaurant. Excitement coursed through her veins. She finally exhaled.

Chapter 34

"Please don't tease me."

Tommy took Shasta's hand and lifted her from the chair. Shasta didn't know what to expect but as Tommy lowered his head and brought his sweet, warm mouth to hers, she knew this was exactly what she sought and yearned for. He tasted sweet, like chocolate mint. He leaned her back and deepened the kiss. Shasta moaned. Tommy's tongue snaked its way into her mouth and Shasta tried to impale hers with his. She reached up and threw her arms around his neck, it was mostly to steady herself. Her legs felt like jelly and thankfully she hadn't fallen. Tommy was creating this sensational hot feeling in the pit of her stomach that she never wanted to end. She loved the taste of him, the smell of him. His hot mouth, his warm skin and his touch was driving her crazy.

Tommy lifted her top to just above her navel and began to caress the soft, warm skin there. He broke contact with her mouth to bathe her neck in kisses. Shasta gripped his shoulders and when Tommy backed her against the table and dipped her over it so that her hair touched the table, pure excitement and adrenaline raced through her veins.

Tommy's tongue found her navel and it dipped in an out, causing Shasta to thrush on the table. Tommy didn't want their first time to be rushed or for someone to come to the door and discover them that way. He lowered her shirt and lifted her off the table. Shasta opened her eyes with confusion. Why did he stop?

"Why did you stop? It felt so good. It felt good to you too, didn't it? I don't know... maybe..."

"I stopped because we should be somewhere more intimate than this diner. I got caught up in the feeling but I want to feel you, all of you. This isn't the place for that but I know a place that is." Shasta smiled inwardly. She knew where he was taking her.

Not ten minutes later, she lay on Tommy's bed in his bedroom. She had briefly seen the downstairs and what she could see was lovely. Tommy lived in a huge five bedroom, four bathroom home. It was a bachelor's dream but Shasta's mind was on other things. Like Tommy taking off his shirt to reveal his sexy, hairless chest. His body was caramel, lean and scrumptious. He lowered himself on her and immediately got down to business. His lips were everywhere there was flesh. He started with her mouth that he completely ravished. His tongue dueled with hers for endless minutes and Shasta knew utter and complete bliss.

She was beyond aroused. She began to move underneath him. She could feel his hardness poking her thigh. She rubbed him through his jeans causing Tommy to groan. Shasta smiled. She was glad that she was getting to him. Tommy lifted her shirt and feasted his eyes on her loveliness. He unhooked her bra and tossed it over the bed and onto the floor. He filled his hands with her loveliness and gloried in the weight of her young, supple breasts. He took one breast into his mouth and sucked it. The nipple grew hard instantly. As he sucked the one breast, his other hand flicked over the nipple of the other breast repeatedly, causing Shasta to arch her back in ecstasy.

Tommy's other hand left her softness and traveled down to the button of her jeans. In no time, Tommy took her jeans off and soon Shasta was only clad in her pink lace underwear. Tommy's hot mouth traced a heated path to her navel bathing her body with his tongue. His right hand pulled down her panties and they went flying to the floor. He leaned back and took in her loveliness. Passion shown in his eyes and Shasta knew the same passion had to be mirrored in hers.

"My beautiful sexy Shasta Brown, you have no idea how many nights I've dreamed of you lying like this in my bed. My vision wasn't anything close to the real thing. Not even close. You are simply breathtaking."

Before Shasta could respond, Tommy was already seeking for his desired treasure. He inserted one sure finger into her heated cove and felt her pulse on his finger. He gloried in her wetness. He played with her clit, while watching Shasta thrush about on the bed. He inserted another finger and finger fucked her to an unknown rhythm. Shasta moaned. She was going insane. He inserted the third finger and strummed her like a violin. Shasta started moaning uncontrollably. She arched her back and grabbed at the sheets. Tommy was bringing her so much pleasure. She couldn't stop herself. She came. Tommy gave a low chuckle and brought his fingers to his mouth and sucked them. Shasta watched in awe and fascination.

"You taste better than any dessert I've ever had. Rich, creamy, and sugary sweet," Shasta leaned forward and took Tommy's mouth in a deep, cleansing kiss. Tommy deepened the kiss but lowered her onto the bed. His mouth left hers and traveled to her heated treasure cove. Shasta closed her eyes and prepared for the adventure. The moment Tommy's tongue touched her hot spot she knew this was a journey she'd never been on before. His tongue was like a forked snake and she literally could feel it snake and curve around her clit. It dashed in and out repeatedly. His tongue thrust deep into her core and Shasta began to scream Tommy's name.

"Tommy! Tommy! Oh, oh...oh, my God. Please....ahhh!!!" Tommy didn't stop but increased his tongue thrusting if that were possible. Shasta grabbed his head and pushed. She wanted his tongue buried in her treasure cove. She moaned her pleasure and screamed his name again and she felt it. She came. She collapsed back on the bed but Tommy was far from being through with her. He flipped her over and shed his jeans. Shasta lay on her stomach and soon felt Tommy's hand resting in the curve of her back. He positioned her the way he wanted and suck his finger into her wet haven and stroked her kitty. Shasta moaned as Tommy lifted her, scooted underneath her and lowered her onto his chest. He positioned her over his mouth and sucked her sweet nectar. He tried to drain the well but he couldn't. He sampled her sweetness to distraction and quickly slid from underneath her.

Shasta was panting when Tommy entered her. He did it with such precision and mastering. From that moment on, she knew money wasn't the only reason Veronica constantly came sniffing around. She'd be crazy not to miss this. It was too good. Shasta was being slowly driven insane as Tommy blew her back out. He thrust forward again and again, in and out repeatedly and Shasta felt like she was on a merry-go-round. She wanted to stay on this ride and never get off.

Tommy watched as Shasta's butt bounced and rebounded. He grunted and groaned. He enjoyed watching her ass shake. He pumped harder and had to hold himself in check. It had been a long time since he was with a woman and he knew he had to pace himself. He didn't want to disappoint Shasta. She deserved so much better than what she had gotten in the past. He wanted to show her that things could be good. He wanted to take her to new heights and fly her to the moon.

He delivered several more deliberate pumps sending Shasta over the edge. “Please, don't stop...ahh, ahh. Tommy!” She screamed and Tommy flipped her over so that she laying her on her back. Shasta's panting was becoming ragged but Tommy had more ground to cover. He kissed her neck and the hills of her breasts before taking one elongated nipple into his mouth and sucking hard. Shasta moaned. He paid homage to the other breast and entered her smoothly. Shasta looked down at Tommy's penis. Nearly half was still sticking out. Seth definitely had nothing on Tommy.

Tommy was hung like a donkey. She couldn't believe all that was up in her! Soon she didn't have time to think of the size of Tommy's stick because that stick was shooting her out into ecstasy. Tommy lifted her body off the bed and took her over to the wall. He had her ass cheeks pressed against the cool wall but she didn't care. She met him stroke for stroke and thrust for powerful thrust as he held her in mid air and made her kitty purr!

Tommy took her back to the bed and placed her on top of him. Shasta was thankful because now she could take control. She rode that magic stick and took Tommy on a pleasure ride. They rode through grassy fields, frost filled mountains, chilly streams and many hills and valleys. They passed a creek and drank from its running water. They passed a cave and briefly took shelter. They passed a brook and frolicked through the water but when Shasta reached the mountain peak, there was no holding back. She leaned all the way back on that magic stick until her hands reached Tommy's knees and twerked her twat, twisting and grinding and shaking his balls. She stroked that stick and squeezed his balls, never losing her rhythm. As she ground deep into Tommy's hips, Tommy grunted and groaned. Shasta could hear his irregular breathing and started grinding even harder. She moaned and panted. She leaned back once more, grinding deep and then she came. Tommy followed shortly behind her, with her name on his lips.

Chapter 35

For the past two days Shasta was on cloud nine. Her thoughts of Seth quickly vanished. She stayed at Tommy's house since the day they made love. Cousin Becky said her place was always open, but she knew Shasta found a home elsewhere.

Shasta dreaded going back to the apartment but she needed to get a few things. Cousin Becky assured her waiting to go was a good idea. She was on her lunch break and what better time to go but now. She still had her key and figured Seth wasn't home. After she gathered her things she'd place the key on the table and would lock the bottom lock. That way Seth knew she'd come by and that was the end of their relationship.

The old smell of the apartment brought up the old memories she and Seth shared. She couldn't help but smile when she put her key in the door. She knew she was one step closer to leaving Seth for good.

The apartment was quiet, just as she expected. Seth did very little to change to the place. She went into the bedroom and noticed someone was in the bed. Shasta did a double take.

"Hey babe, why are you here so early? You just left." Shannon lifted her head up and to her surprise Seth wasn't standing in the room with her.

"How dare you?" Shasta scoffed. She gathered her things. "There's so much I could do to you right now but my life has been amazing since I last left this apartment, so I refuse to let you ruin my day."

"I'm sorry. I don't want you to think this was intentional...." Shannon pleaded.

"You're not sorry and neither is Seth. You're sorry because you got caught. You and Seth can have each other. I moved on and tell him he don't have to worry about me from this day forward." Shasta took the key out of her pocket and threw it at Shannon. "Here's your spare key tramp!"

Shasta knew she couldn't leave without relieving some stress. She walked out the room while Shannon stayed in bed. Shasta filled a glass of water and threw it at Shannon.

"Why don't you take a bath tramp, this is probably the only water you had on your body for weeks!"

"I can't believe..."

"Believe it! I can't believe you'd mess with someone who's taken. How dare you sleep in the very bed me and Seth made love in? How could you sleep at night?"

Shasta didn't wait for an answer. She picked up her bag and gathered the rest of her things and left the apartment. Just as she walked out the building Seth parked his moped on the sidewalk near the door.

"Shasta." He called out. She turned around and shook her head. She walked as fast as her legs could carry her back to the diner.

"Wait," Seth ran past her and stopped in front of her. "So you thought you could leave without saying bye."

"Get away from me!" Shasta shouted. "I have nothing to say to you, you and your little tramp can continue on with your life."

Shasta brushed past Seth and rolled her eyes.

"Shasta, I never intended to hurt you."

"Yeah and I never intended to be hurt. I gave you everything. I trusted you and you took advantage of my heart." Shasta yelled over the loud cars passing by on the street. The honking didn't make it any better for her to communicate to Seth, not that she wanted to.

"I know, and like I mentioned before I do apologize. I didn't think things were going to end up this way. I adore you, you were my queen. But..."

"But you got caught. Don't give me the whole soppy story. Seth do me a favor, you go your way and

I'll go mine. I came to get my belongings and I wanted to do it without running into you. This is a big city with a lot people. I'm certain that it won't take long to get over you."

Shasta walked down the street and didn't dare turn back. She felt relieved and confident. She didn't expect to see Seth but at least she got to say what she wanted to him. She smiled walking back to the diner. She was in the mood to see Tommy's sexy face. She wanted more of him and was glad Seth was nothing but a memory.

******

"I don't know what he expected from me but I'm so glad that is over." Shasta explained her running into Seth and his tramp to Cousin Becky.

"I bet that girl was upset you threw water on her. I bet that took a lot out of you." Cousin Becky rolled out some dough. She was glad Shasta came back when she did. She was getting lonely talking to herself.

"It didn't take me out of character, it made me feel good. I had anger in my heart and watching that water hit Shannon's face was comical. Running into Seth was even better. The look on his face when I showed my attitude," she shook her head. "He didn't know what to do."

"Most guys don't. Women are so quick to please their men it's sickening. But when we show an ugly side…they don't know how to handle it. But enough about him, I'm glad that is over with. How are things going with you and Tommy?"

Shasta's smile was as bright as the sun. "It's been lovely."

"I bet because you got him smiling all over the diner. He's giving special deals left and right. You must have some power in between those frail legs."

"Cousin Becky!" Shasta shouted.

"What, it's clear you gave him some cookie. The way you too look at each other, I know he wants to close the diner down for a few hours and take you in the back and…"

"Ok ,ok ,ok, you're right. I love it!" She exclaimed. "It's nothing I've ever experience before. The love making is so passionate and he's so into me. I can tell and feel it."

"I bet you can." Cousin Becky giggled. "On a serious note, you think you are going to live with him permanently?"

"I don't know. I've been thinking about it. I know he'd take good care of me. I can only imagine that, but I don't want to go down the same path I did with Seth. What if Veronica comes back? I know he has a protective order against her but that eventually goes away. They had a relationship and he was due to marry her. I want to be sure he's done with her."

"Oh trust me sweetheart he's done with her." Cousin Becky stated. "One thing I do know about Tommy is this, he's not going to mess around with a lot of females. It's not good for business and he never wants that kind of drama around the diner. He is a one woman man and if he let you into his home, then you are there to stay, unless you pull a Veronica.

"I don't plan on doing that. But I want some things to change. I need to have something in my name. I need to have a sense of security for when things go wrong. I don't expect Tommy to cheat on me but you never know. What if the worst happens and I have to show proof that my name is on the place."

"You have a good point, just talk to him about it. Tommy is open to anything and with him knowing what happened in your recent past, he'll take that into consideration." She assured Shasta. "And I'm not saying this because he's my cousin. I'm telling you this because I know him. He's a damn good man."

"Yeah, I think I'm going to talk to him after we get off work. I know it's just the beginning but under the crazy circumstances, it's causing me to move a bit fast. I don't want to live out on the streets Cousin Becky. I can't do dumpsters and restaurant bathrooms."

"Oh child please, you won't be homeless. You still got me. Just think things can only go up from here. Stop being so negative and start celebrating the future." Cousin Becky placed the filling into the pie and made her crust to go over top of the pie.

Shasta felt a lecture coming on. She got herself ready for Cousin Becky to rant on about relationships and life. Shasta knew as long as she nodded and agreed at the right times she could daydream about Tommy's sexy physique.

Chapter 36

Shasta took the last of the sweet potato pies out the oven. She was pouring fresh lemonade into the huge tumbler pitcher when Tommy came into the kitchen. Shasta had her back to him and Cousin Becky. Cousin Becky noted the gleamor in his eyes and she took off her apron and tossed it on the table. She gave Tommy a loving nudge as she left the kitchen.

Shasta went on working and added sugar to the huge green pitcher of lemonade. They were close to being out and she wanted to make a fresh pitcher for the evening. It was only four-thirty but everything needed to be ready for the dinner diners. She stopped stirring the lemonade and sighed. Tommy was near. She could smell his heady cologne. She turned and noticed him a few feet away from her.

"Look at you slaving away in this hot kitchen. Are you thirsty? You look like you could use a cool drink." Shasta wiped her brow and realized she was warm. She intended to grab a glass of the fresh lemonade when Tommy stilled her hand.

"I got just the drink for you but it's out in the dining area. Come on and have a drink with me." Shasta looked askance at Tommy but quickly nodded her head. Her heart was overflowing with anticipation. As soon as Tommy opened the kitchen door, she smelled roses as she followed him from the kitchen. She was in awe as she eyed the seven or eight dozen roses strategically placed throughout the diner. Red, pink, and white roses immersed the diner. They were so beautiful. White vanilla scented candles nearly equaled to the number of roses, also lighted a path that led to a huge heart shaped mattress positioned adjacent to the counter. Pink and red rose petals formed a perfect heart in the center and Shasta could feel her eyes well up with tears. She'd never seen anything so lovely in her entire life. It was all for her. The enormity of it all came crashing down on her and she could no longer hold her tears in. They streamed down her face and Tommy wiped each one of them away with his warm fingers.

"I hope those are happy tears." He gently took Shasta by the hand and led her to a table that was so romantically set that Shasta cried all over again. There were roses in the center in an oversize glass vase with a red ribbon around it. A bottle of chilled champagne sat to the right and two huge silver servers sat to the left, along with two 24 karat gold plated wine glasses. Shasta was so overjoyed her body shook.

"Hey, if you keep acting like that, I'm going to think you don't like it. You do like it don't you?" Shasta thought it was a silly question. She loved it! She just was so shaken. Nothing like this had ever happened to her. This was like something out of one of her dreams.

"I love it ! It's amazing. When did you have time to do this? Where is everyone?" Shasta looked around and noticed all the blinds were closed. She bet money the door was locked and the closed sign was flipped over. Shawna, Antoinette, and Becky were gone too. Tommy closed the diner early. He must've had this planned all along.

"Oh my God, you sent everyone home. I haven't seen you most of the day...." It dawn on her that he got everything together while she was in the kitchen. Shasta smiled and pulled Tommy toward her.

"So you are happy. Good. Now let's have that drink." Tommy reached into the basket holding the champagne and popped the cork. The top went flying and some champagne dropped to the floor. Shasta let out a whoop of laughter and Tommy spun her around in a circle and kissed her deeply. She knew right then and there, that she found the love she sought.

****

After a delicious succulent meal of beef burgundy over seasoned pepper rice, string beans, homemade buttered dinner rolls, rich pecan pie and two glasses of the heady champagne, Shasta was in heaven. She couldn't believe Tommy had done this all for her. The roses, the candles, the huge heart shaped bed and the dinner had to take some planning. When had he planned it all? When did he have time?

"When did you plan all of this? How did you get everything here?" Shasta asked, taking another sip of wine. Tommy watched her and decided to let the cat out of the bag. Before long, she'd find out anyway and he wanted to be the one to tell her. She wasn't like Veronica and her intentions were pure. She wanted to be loved like he did with no restraints and no ulterior motives. He took a deep breath and silently prayed for the best.

"By now you've probably heard about how hard I worked to get this place off the ground. You've probably heard it's a family owned business and I only hire family, until you...what you more than likely haven't heard about is my parental background. My mother died when I was quite young and my family here took me in. I don't have any siblings so the family didn't mind much. I've been told I was a good kid and even I can remember how the family seemed to dote on me but..."

"What about your father, did you know him? Did he know you?" Shasta took Tommy's hand. He kissed her knuckles and continued speaking.

"I knew of him. I saw him maybe four times a year, five if I was lucky. My father was a world traveler...in fact he was pretty awesome. He was a singer. Your parents may have heard of him. His Song 'It's All in the Game' was composed by vice president Charles Dawes in 1912 and the lyrics were later written by Carl Sigman in 1951. That single was so fly, it got number one on the R&B charts and sold over 3.5 million copies globally. Even though my father went on to record other songs like 'That Chick's too Young to Fry', none came close to achieving the success of 'It's All in the Game', a doo whoop song. I heard it on the radio today. My heart swelled with pride too. That's my Dad, I always say. Well in 1968 my old man died of a brain aneurysm in Henrico Country, Virginia. He was only 47." Tommy finished his spiel and noticed Shasta wiping away tears.

Her tears meant something to him. They weren't for show like Veronica's and her compassion made Tommy realize he'd fallen in love. Wow, that little siren from Virginia had captured his heart. His heart let out a huge sigh. She was the one he'd searched for.

"Tommy, I'm so sorry. To lose both of your parents...." Shasta really began crying in earnest now. She felt for him. She and her mom weren't always on good terms but if her head was cold, she couldn't even think of it.

"Hey now, today is about happiness and celebration. We are celebrating us. No more tears okay. Okay." Shasta nodded, sniffling and Tommy grabbed a few Kleenex tissues off the counter and handed them to her. Shasta smiled through her tears. Tommy wasn't finished with his story. She wanted him to continue.

"Go ahead, I won't interrupt again." Shasta said but Tommy wasn't even worried. If he told Veronica the story, she'd would've asked about his inheritance and found ways to obtain it from him. Greed was Veronica's middle name and her mission of getting money from Tommy was always obvious.

"Since I'm an only child I received a sizable inheritance, a trust fund if you will. I couldn't touch that money until I turned 25. My father died the year before my twenty-fifth birthday and needless to say, Veronica was already circling long before then. She didn't know how much exactly I'd receive but she knew it was far more than her eyes ever laid on." Tommy paused for a moment, as if going down merry lane was painful to him. Shasta leaned over and brushed her lips with his, bringing a smile to his handsome face.

"Veronica heard through the grapevine my father was worth over twelve million dollars. It was a rumor of course but she ran with it. She even had me convinced at one point that I would inherit half of it. I didn't, but my inheritance was nothing to cry about. Between the insurance money and my trust, I was indeed a worthy man, raking in almost five million dollars. The diner was up and running before then and making good money.

I still got residuals off my father's music and had inherited his estate. The home I live in now belonged to my father. Veronica was more overjoyed in my inheritance or winnings as she'd call it than I was. My father was gone and I was still grieving but she said I should celebrate my good fortune. She said that if my father didn't want me to have the money, he wouldn't have left it to me. I suppose that was true so, not even a month after my father passed away, I let V convince me to take her to Vegas. I was such a fool. She drank and drank some more, then she left me and wend up in bed with some rich brotha from up north." Shasta gave a startled cry. Her mouth formed a perfect 'O'. How she could do that to him? Was she crazy or just mean? Shasta knew she promised not to interrupt but she couldn't help herself.

"How could she do that to you?! How dare her. She didn't deserve you. She deserves someone like her." As soon as Shasta said it, Tommy knew she was right. Veronica deserved someone as spineless and despicable as she was. He hoped she found that somebody because he was through with her. There was no turning back especially since he had what he wanted most. His soul mate. He decided to finish his story.

"V wandered off after I wouldn't give her any more money. She had already blew over five grand on machines and shopping. I told her after we had a nice dinner, we'd cuddle and wake up the next morning and hit the town. She didn't want to wait until the next day. She wanted what she wanted immediately. I searched for her for two days. It was like she had vanished. On the afternoon of the second day, I caught her sneaking out one of the presidential suites on the thirteenth floor. Apparently someone had granted her every wish that I couldn't fulfill."

"She cheated on you with a stranger?"

"He wasn't just any stranger; he co-owned two hotels in Vegas and owned several boutiques. He had money and V always did flock to the fellas with the dollars. I was just a lowly diner owner whose dad was famous. Besides, it wasn't her first time cheating on me. I saw her creeping out and we argued. I left her in Vegas and returned home, heartbroken. It has been that way for a long time, until now."

This man was so amazing. He treated her like royalty, making her want to give so much back to him in return. His story inspired her. She saw how people of her race could overcome. She wasn't rich and didn't have any money but she knew what she could do. She would be all that Tommy deserved and much more.

Chapter 37

Shasta laid in the center of the heart shaped bed. Tommy never did tell her how the bed gotten there and how he managed to get everything together for their enchanted evening without her knowledge, but she no longer cared. She cared about this moment and all the other moments they shared. Seth came into her life when she desperately wanted and needed love, yet he didn't love her. She realized she really didn't love him either.

She wanted so desperately what she saw in movies, on the streets and in stores and restaurants. She thought she knew what love was but compared to what she experienced with Tommy, Seth didn't come close, not even a little bit. She didn't have to go hide up in some tree with Tommy for fear of being lynched. No one held a loaded shot gun at her chest or proclaimed her a whore for wanting him.

She and Tommy belonged together. She felt in her heart that Tommy was her soul mate. Adoration, respect, joy and belonging felt real in this relationship. She'd never hurt Tommy the way Veronica did. She truthfully thanked Veronica silently for sending her the man of her dreams.

When she looked into Tommy's eyes ,her whole heart melted. She had denied herself this because of Seth.

She had fought it and hard but she loved this man. She wasn't surprised. The feeling had been coming on for quite some time, yet they both needed healing. They were quite the pair of bandaged hearts. Their broken hearts led them to each other and Shasta loved every minute of it.

Shasta started unbuttoning Tommy's shirt and pulled it down his arms. His masculine body was so inviting. Shasta started kissing her way across one shoulder blade before returning the favor to the other one. She nipped the skin above Tommy's male nipple, causing him to groan. Her tongue laved the spot and then found his nipple. She traced circles around its hardness and she caressed Tommy through his dress pants.

Tommy groaned in earnest but Shasta wanted to be in charge. She pushed Tommy onto the bed, causing him to lie on his back. She kissed him deeply and pressed her short pink tongue into his mouth. Tommy caressed her breasts through her blouse causing Shasta to moan in his mouth. She broke feel of Tommy's hot mouth to rain kisses all over his chest. She gloried in his sexy, strong physique. He was magnificently built. Her eyes fell to the imprint in his slacks. She sighed in anticipation of what she knew was next but first she wanted to please her man.

She unbuttoned his pants and unzipped the zipper of his slacks. Tommy's eyes flew open but Shasta was much too busy to notice. She reached inside and found her joystick. Tommy was hot, hard, and ready. Shasta's hand strummed over that joystick like BeBe King himself had possessed her. Tommy's breathing became ragged but Shasta didn't lose focus. She pulled her long magic wand out of hiding and wrapped her mouth around its wide base. Tommy muttered something incoherent and Shasta opened her mouth wider, to take him all in. She squeezed his balls and sucked that stick like a pro. Tommy murmured something only he understood but Shasta knew she was in control. She continued to pleasure him, driving Tommy insane. She got up for air just long enough to take off her pants, panties and blouse.

Tommy was zoned out when she got on top of him. She guided his magic stick into her hot cove with ease and rode that joystick like it was no tomorrow. Tommy caught up with her and pulled one breast free from her bra and sucked on her nipple. Shasta moaned when Tommy leaned forward and gripped her butt, rocking with her and grinding his pelvis deep into hers. She continued her assault but she was getting raked over the coals as well. Tommy was no slouch in the bedroom and when he lifted her high into the air and delivered several powerful pumps while standing against the counter, Shasta came with a flourish. Tommy came too; smoke signaling all was well in both their worlds.

****

Shasta was in awe from the way things went last night. Tommy assured her taking a break today from the diner was needed. She knew things were going in the right direction yet something was missing. Seth existence played so little in her mind that she almost chuckled when she thought of him. She got up from bed, made a cup of tea and sat on the sofa.

She turned the television on and scanned through the channels. All this happiness and for some reason she still felt alone. She had no one to talk to although Cousin Becky was the only one she ran to. She wanted to talk to one of her old friends but she had none. There was no one to call, no one to share the good news to about her and Seth's breakup. She wanted to talk to Cassie, a voice she longed for. She missed her family, Tommy had his with him. Why couldn't she have the same? She knew she had to risk it, calling Cassie was the only solution to her missing her family.

The phone rang, Shasta patiently clutched onto the phone. Her grip was tight as she swayed left in right on the sofa. Cassie's sweet voice answered the phone and Shasta's heart dropped. It had been over ten months since she heard her sister's voice.

"Hello?" Cassie sounded annoyed.

"Hi." Shasta whispered.

"Shasta is that you?" Cassie cried out.

"Yes, yes it's me. How are you doing ?"

"Excited now that you called." Cassie sounded relieved. Shasta heard the happiness in her voice which caused her to be happy.

"I'm sorry for all the drama I caused, but I really wanted to be loved. You got the letter right? The one I sent."

"Yes and I've held onto it ever since. I didn't tell Momma you reached out to me. It's really good to hear from you Shasta...wow."

"Yeah, and guess what, not only am I working at the diner but..."

"What?" Cassie asked.

"I'm dating the owner of the diner."

"The black guy, the one you mentioned in your letter? You done went back to black!" Cassie exclaimed. "I knew you'd get out of that phase. So what's New York like?" Cassie was intrigued.

"It's a big city Cassie. Oh my there are tall buildings and there are so many people here. More than I've ever seen in my life. It's nothing like back home, how's everything at home by the way?" Shasta asked.

Cassie couldn't believe she was talking to her sister. She couldn't believe after all these months she decided to call her. "Things calmed down a few months after you left. People realized you and Seth weren't coming back. There's still a few arguments here...oh for we black folks there's less jobs. Ever since the romance between the two of you, whites are refusing to hire blacks. It's been crazy down here. We black folks have to go out of town just to get a job now! Momma is doing alright though, she still in church every Sunday praying you get your life together."

"Well you can tell her those prayers have been answered."

"Oh I will first thing after I get off this phone. She really misses you. One night she didn't know I came over here. She was crying on her knees begging God to assure your safety. And on her kitchen table were letters. She wrote you a letter each day but didn't have an address to send them to. I know she misses you and regrets the argument. She believes she forced you out of Virginia."

"She did, and a thousand others. I don't regret anything that I did though. If I didn't leave Virginia and come to New York I wouldn't have met Tommy. He's a really nice guy. I mean it too, he protects me and he makes me feel loved. I always wanted that feeling of being cherished. I use to get jealous of you because I never knew what it felt like. It feels good Cassie…it feels so good."

"It does. I can't describe it but once you know the feeling of love, you don't ever want it to go away. I am happy for you Shasta, I really am." Cassie said.

"Thank you."

"So what's he like?"

"He's tall…creamy caramel…and handsome!" Shasta blushed as she reminisced on their nights together.

"Hmm, you think you ever going to come home and bring him to Momma?"

"I don't know. I miss home so much. I really do. But what are people going to say to me? Everyone knew I dealt with Seth. I don't want to start any drama if I come down there. Maybe you and Momma can come up here. Tommy has a nice house, enough room for all of you to come and visit."

"That sounds like a good idea. But that's going to take a lot of convincing Momma. She misses you a lot, but I don't know if she'd travel up to New York."

"She will, I plan on calling her soon. Hopefully she answers."

"I'm sure she will. So what are you going to do now?" Cassie asked.

"Nothing, I took the day off to rest. I needed it. I've been working at the diner slaving in that kitchen. I'm making good money but people who work hard still need a day of rest. I think I'm going to look at some shows, relax and wait for my man to come on home."

Cassie giggled. "It sure feels good to hear your voice."

"Thank you, I feel the same way. I don't miss Seth one bit." Shasta confessed.

"I don't blame you."

"I really don't. Once he showed his true colors I knew the relationship was over. I was sad. I cried so much, to the point where I knew no more tears could fall out. I loved him, or at least thought I did. He promised he'd never leave or hurt me, which he broke the two promises. I trusted Seth with every ounce of me. I never thought he'd do me the way he did." Shasta shook her head and closed her eyes.

"It's all the past now."

"It sure is and I'm so so happy."

The two girls giggled. Cassie talked to Shasta about her job and what she planned on doing if she and momma came to New York. Shasta was filling in the void that was missing. She was glad to talk to Cassie and catch up. She sincerely missed her family.

****

A week went by and Shasta still hadn't talked to her Momma like she intended. Since she returned to work, business had gotten hectic. The diner was busy from the moment she put her apron on, to the moment she took it off. Once Shasta got home, Tommy wanted to make love and it was so good that they'd fall asleep in each others arms. She knew calling Momma was important and still wanted them to come and visit.

"Good morning to you sunshine." Cousin Becky said as Shasta walked into the room.

"Good morning. How was your night?"

"Oh it was darling. I got the rest I needed and my husband caressed these here toes of mine." She grinned from ear to ear. "Are you ready to work hard again?"

"Do I have a choice?" Shasta scoffed but laughed.

"Good question. I don't think so. Go ahead and hand me those muffins over there. We are going to get hit pretty hard this morning. Saturdays are the busiest days of the week. Everyone wants to go out, shop and eat." Cousin Becky explained. "Where's Tommy?" She asked as she put the muffins in the oven.

"He's up front cleaning the floors and waiting for the girls to come in."

"Oh ok, how are things with you two going? You still on cloud nine?"

"Oh you know I am. I look at Tommy and believe I'm the luckiest girl in the world. I have a man who adores me and says exactly what he means. He takes me out to the picture shows and treats me like a queen. But there's one thing missing."

"What, a baby? Don't tell me you want to be pregnant now."

"Oh no...heavens no! I'd want a wedding before any children. What's missing is my family. What use is it if you can't enjoy your happiness with family?"

"I agree...well have you talked to them?"

"I called my sister last week. She said things have changed a bit since Seth and I left. She said there are no jobs for blacks anymore. They all have to go out of the town to get a job. It's insane but I want to go back, but I think it's best for them to come up here."

"I think that's a good idea too. I don't want you going down there and they do something to you.

Besides Tommy wouldn't let you go alone and if someone said anything crazy to you, he'd flip."

"I know, so I talked to my sister about coming here. I want her and Momma to see how I'm living. I think that'd be great don't you?"

"Of course, and they could stay at Tommy's place with you since it's big enough."

"Right, that's what I was telling Cassie."

"Then they could eat this good ol' food here."

"Yeah and I know Momma would want to show you a thing or two." Shasta got excited.

"Oh I don't mind, I could always use a secret or two for our loyal customers." Cousin Becky noticed Tommy peeping his head in. She winked at him while Shasta was talking and he smiled back. She knew Tommy overheard their conversation and was going to put Shasta's idea to a reality.

"Why don't you give your mom a call when you get off work? That way you two can talk for as long as you want." Cousin Becky knew Tommy heard what she said. She was happy for Shasta and wanted for her to see her family as much as she did.

Chapter 38

Shasta took a deep breath and picked up the receiver. She knew her Momma should be home by now. It was going on nine o'clock in Viriginia and her mother probably was about to draw her bath water. Shasta closed her eyes for a brief minute and dialed the number.

After three rings, she heard the voice she thought she wouldn't hear ever again. Shasta exhaled and savored the sound. She knew she was at fault for a lot that went on, they both were but she couldn't imagine being like Tommy with no parents or siblings. She knew in that, she would never want to trade places with him.

"Hello, hello. Who is this?"

"Momma," Shasta could only get out the one word. She was so emotional. She could feel the tears well up in her eyes but she refused to let them fall.

"Shasta...Shasta. Is that you, baby?" Shasta did allow a few tears to escape. She called her baby. Maybe all was not lost after all.

"Momma, it's me. I'm still your baby girl." Shasta smiled through her tears and waited for her Momma to speak.

"You've been gone a long time but I could never forget your voice. You're my child. Nothing has happened to you has it?" For the next few minutes, Shasta filled her mother in on Seth, Emily/Shannon and finding a new job. She purposely left out Tommy. She wanted to save the best part for last.

"Cassie told me she talked to you, said you got a new job and a black boss. Does he know about you and that white boy? We've had a big fall out here since you two left. I was able to keep my job but Cassie and Derek along with many others lost their jobs and work counties away from their homes. It's madness, I tell you."

Shasta was glad Cassie didn't tell Momma about Tommy. Yet she did feel bad for all of them essentially, because of her and Seth, many of the town folk had to uproot and look for work elsewhere.

"I'm sorry to hear about that Momma. I never knew it would get so crazy there. I never knew that because I wanted to be loved, so many people would suffer. It's not fair...." Shasta cried and to her surprise, Momma soothed her through the phone.

"There, there child. What's done is done. That white boy showed his true colors to you and it's over. Maybe in a different town or time; things could have been different for the two of you but you got to put all that behind you now. You can start a new life now. As much as I'll miss you, home is not the place for you to be. Not now anyways. These folks here hold grudges and act like the two of you left last week instead of over ten months ago. No child, home is not the answer."

"Well what if you and Cassie came here?" Shasta said before she realized what she was saying. Could she even afford that? She had saved some money since Tommy wouldn't let her buy anything. He took care of all her needs, personally and physically. She nearly had five hundred dollars saved. That should cover them for the trip and the things they would need there. At least she hoped so.

"Girl, what you talking about? We can't come there. I don't have money for no trip and Cassie is strapped and who gonna pay for it, that boss of yours?" Momma said with a laugh but a light bulb went off in Shasta's head. Maybe that wasn't such a bad idea. Since she was living with Tommy rent free, maybe he could pay for them to come and if it was more than the five hundred or so that she had saved, she could pay him back later.

She was so engrossed in her train of thought she didn't realize Tommy was standing in the doorway of the bedroom. When she finally looked up and caught his eye, what she saw there she knew had to be mirrored in her own eyes. She loved this man. She smiled and he walked over to her. He motioned for her to set the phone down and whispered in her ear. Shasta's eyes lit up and she smiled through tears. She kissed him deeply, caressed his cheek and picked up the phone. She would get her wish after all.

"Momma tell Cassie to pack her bags and you pack yours too. Ya'll flying out to New York City as soon as I make the reservations."

****

Of course Momma wanted to know what was going on and how she could afford the tickets. Then there was the issue of Momma and Cassie never being on an airplane. By the end of the call, Shasta's mind was spinning. After all the arrangements were scheduled, Shasta realized she never got to tell Momma about Tommy. Tommy. That handsome, amazing man was too much. What he whispered in her ear so intimately was these seven words. 'Let me make this happen for you". She wanted to tell Momma about the new man in her life but she knew Momma would learn soon enough.

What she felt for this man, she didn't have to hide. The love she felt for him was shown openly for the world to see. The diner customers were in awe of the two of them. Uncle Titus stopped in often to see the happy couple. Some female customers said wedding bells were in the air, while the men openly told Tommy how much they admired that she was not a gold digging persona like Veronica. She and Tommy never said much but looked at each other and smiled. Many days the diner closed early because what they wanted to do to each other needed no audience.

Cousin Becky laughed the next morning as she put some pies in the oven. Sometimes she'd say, 'You two keep doing that nasty, I'm gonna have me a great cousin on the way, or say 'Don't worry, when y'all on y'alls second honeymoon, I'll watch the twins.' Having gotten used to her talk, Shasta would laugh and shake her head. She was happy. The folks here cared about each other. They applauded your successes and lent a hand when you failed. She belonged here. The people showed her each day she did. It was an exhilarating feeling. She sensed a change in Tommy. She felt like he was ready to pop the question but she wouldn't push him.

Her patience would hold on for as long as it took. He was definitely something worth waiting for. She sighed her happiness and prepared for Momma's visit. She vowed to make this trip memorable and Becky decided to lend her a hand in doing that. The diner would be closed at four o'clock and they planned to meet up at Tommy's and Shasta would introduce Tommy to her mother.

Shasta took Tommy's car to pick them up, and Tommy stayed behind to get the diner ready for closing. Their flight came in at 2:45 and as the time approached, she felt herself getting antsy. It was so crucial that everything was right. The house was gorgeously decorated and everything was perfectly placed. The two guestrooms were tastefully decorated in Momma and Cassie's favorite colors. The gourmet kitchen was laid out with fresh fruits and nuts and homemade apple cider like Momma used to make. It wasn't holiday time but it felt that way to her.

She helped Cousin Becky prepare the meal. It was all Mommas' favorites. Of course many of the food Cousin Becky prepared was already some of Momma's favorites but Shasta added a few more to the list.

After assuring everything was set. Shasta checked the time. It was a quarter til two. She grabbed Tommy's keys off the counter and headed to the airport. Determined not to let nerves overcome her, she put her foot to the pedal. She arrived a little after two at the terminal. She sighed nervously. Things would be okay. Things would be perfect, they had to be.

Chapter 39

Shasta watched Momma and Cassie's eyes glued to the car window. They all were silent, the only words Shasta heard were ohhh, and ahhhh, and most importantly "Look at that building over there!" Cassie fell in love the moment she stepped off the plane.

Shasta and Momma had an intimate moment when Momma noticed her. She hugged Shasta so tight all of Shasta's worries about the past vanished. Tears flooded down her cheeks and Momma kissed her on her forehead. Shasta smiled as she reminisced on the moment while driving home.

"Wow look at that huge horse!" Cassie shouted, causing Shasta to snap back in reality. She smirked realizing in this very moment her dreams were now a reality.

"So is Mr. handsome going to be at the house?" Cassie asked after Momma told her to stop yelling at every single thing.

"Mr. handsome, so there's another guy?" Momma asked. Cassie covered her mouth when she realized Momma didn't know about Tommy. "Whoops," she made a scared face at Shasta.

"Thanks a lot Cassie." Shasta scoffed.

"Well who is he?" Momma was tired of being out of the loop.

"He's...well he's my boss at the diner. We started talking and after he offered me the job..."

"He wanted more." Cassie butted in.

"Shut up...but yeah, basically." Shasta looked at Momma hoping she didn't get upset. "He got the plane tickets for you two to get up here. He saw how hard it was for me not having you two around."

"That's sweet of him. It's great to have a man who notices the little things in life. Family is important and for him to want you to be around yours says a lot about him. I like him already, now for the serious question. Have you run into Seth?"

That question made Shasta smile, if that was asked to her a few weeks ago she woud have gotten upset. "I haven't run into him but if I do I'm prepared. I'm no longer angry. Actually I'm happy this happened to me. If I hadn't moved to New York with Seth, I never would've met Tommy. And Momma he's the best thing that's ever happened to me. He really is. Every tear in my body was shed purposely and now that those sad tears are gone all I have are happy tears."

"How sweet," Cassie coed, "how far are we from his place?"

"Just a few blocks. Tommy is at work so we won't see him until later tonight. He'd rather that we get acquainted and all settled in before he gets home."

"Home, so you live with him?" Momma caught on to what Shasta was saying.

"We do live together. I was going to move in with Cousin Becky..."

"Who?" Momma asked.

"Cousin Becky, she's Tommy's cousin and she works at the diner. She gives good advice. She didn't care for me being with Seth, she actually said it was a phase and was glad we broke up."

"Good...I like Cousin Becky." Momma commented.

Shasta laughed, "She offered for me to stay at her house but she has a family. There's no need to stay with her when I could stay with Tommy and have peace of mind."

"That's good and all but I want you to be married. It's not okay for you to stay with a man, have sexual relations with him and not be married. I think you need to reconsider."

Shasta didn't want to argue with Momma, in fact she was right. She didn't know how to approach Tommy about the whole marriage thing. She figured it would be too fast but she was certain Momma was going to bring it up to him. Shasta hoped Tommy would understand.

Shasta remained silent and listened to Momma rant on about the importance of marriage. She informed Shasta she didn't want her out in the streets especially since going back to Virginia was forbidden. Thankfully after ten minutes of Momma going on and on, Shasta pulled up to her home.

"This place is huge." Cassie's eyes widened to saucers.

"Yeah." Shasta parked the car and unlocked her door. "Let me show you to your rooms.

Cassie and Momma smiled entering Shasta's new home. The furniture was all up to date and nice. She lived in a clean environment and Momma couldn't help but be inpressed. "You've came a long way." Momma sighed after putting her bags down. "But I still don't approve of this." She mumbled under her breath.

Shasta took Momma's bags and they followed her upstairs. Shasta made sure Momma's and Cassie's room were side by side just in case one wanted to sleep with the other.

"Why don't you two ladies take a shower and get settled in. I bet that plane ride was long and probably a bit disgusting." She scrunched up her face.

"That's true, it sure was. Come on Momma let me see if I can work the shower for you." Cassie winked at Shasta as they walked into the bathroom. Shasta went into the living room and called the diner. She was relieved when Cousin Becky answered the phone.

"Hello." She answered.

"Hey Cousin Becky it's me, Shasta."

"Oh hey boo. Your ma and sis make it in yet?"

"They sure did. When Ma found out Tommy and I were living together she almost flipped and started giving out lectures saying how she wants me to be married first."

"Oh...hmm well she has every right to. You know you two aren't married and from the looks of what happened before, she wants you to be cautious."

"I know, but I wanted to give Tommy a heads up. Knowing Momma she doesn't hold her tongue back. She's going to approach him about marriage. I don't want him getting upset and I don't want Momma to leave New York with an attitude. We just got back on good terms I don't want things to go sour and I..."

"Calm down sweetheart, things are not going to go sour." Cousin Becky stopped Shasta from ranting. She heard the worry in her voice and wanted to assure her things were going to be okay. "Knowing Tommy he's not going to argue with your mother. He's going to talk to her and give her the respect she deserves to have. It's going to be okay. I'm coming over after we get off work. Tommy is going to make dinner and we all are going to have a nice family meal. Don't stress. We will be home in a few hours. In the meantime take your mother and sister out and let them explore the town. Rest assured things are not going to go bad."

Shasta sighed. "Okay thanks Cousin Becky."

"No worries."

"Shasta!" Cassie called out. "How you turn on this shower, it's too fancy for Momma and me!"

Shasta rolled her eyes and walked back upstairs. She knew it would only be moments before she heard Cassie calling for assistance again.

Chapter 40

Shasta was sitting at the dining room table in the huge gourmet kitchen pouring fresh lemonade from the pitcher, when Cassie came in and sat down at the table.

"Sista girl, this place is huge. It's just plain beautiful! That shower was crazy. It felt like a hundred mini hands were caressing my back. It's a shame that I can put my whole bedroom back home in that bathroom. Momma is actually singing in the shower. You hear me, she's singing girl!" Shasta couldn't help but laugh. She too remembered when she had first come to Tommy's house. It was like something out of a magazine. Everything was so tastefully decorated and perfect. You couldn't tell a man lived there.

"I'm glad you like it. This *is* one beautiful place. Wait until you see the grounds..."

"Grounds, are you sure your man don't own more than one diner? This place is like a mansion. I wonder did he have an interior decorator decorate it or did he do it himself."

"Oh, it was one of them decorators. I can tell." Shasta and Cassie turned to see Momma standing in the door way.

"Momma, I thought you were still in the shower." Shasta said, not knowing if she should reveal

Tommy's true identity until he arrived. She didn't want to start talking about him and his life story when he walked through the door. It was a private matter and she could tell losing his parents still hurt him. Momma could sometimes be insensitive with her words.

"Tommy will be here soon and we all can ask him." Shasta said handing Cassie a glass of lemonade. She was pouring Momma a glass when Tommy came through the door with an arm full of bags.

"Hello." Tommy walked over to where they all stood. Tommy smiled and his gaze automatically connected with Shasta, making her blush. She was so happy he was home. Uncle Titus came in with a long silver cart. Shasta noticed the five serving trays and smiled.

Cassie's mouth hung open. Her eyes never left Tommy's as he walked toward Momma. Momma's eyes were in a blank stare until Tommy grabbed her hand and kissed it. She came out of her trace and blinked twice.

"You must be Momma. How very nice to meet you finally. I'm Tommy Edwards. I hope you will enjoy your stay here. If you need anything at all, please don't hesitate to ask."

"Oh... Momma, yes, I must be Momma..." Shasta watched in shock as her mother stumbled over her words. If she wasn't watching with her own eyes, she'd never believe it. Momma was spell bound, and so was Cassie.

"Of course, I'm Momma. I'm her Momma and hers." Momma laughed nervously and Tommy laughed too. Shasta smiled. It seemed that Tommy had that blinding affect on all women, including Momma.

"Why don't you ladies join us in the dining room? I know after a flight like that, you have to be starving." Tommy suggested and Uncle Titus pushed the serving cart and its goodies into the formal dining room.

"Ladies, this is my Uncle Titus. Uncle Titus, this is Momma Brown and Ms. Cassie, Shasta's sister." Uncle Titus and the others exchanged hellos and Uncle Titus left. Shasta figured she should say something to break the ice and she thought of Cousin Becky.

"I thought Cousin Becky was coming by? Cousin Becky is the cook down at the diner." She explained to Momma and Cassie.

"Oh yeah, it would be real nice to meet her. I bet Momma would like to compare dish ideas." Cassie laughed as so did Shasta. Shasta was laughing because her sister had finally closed her mouth.

"That sounds like a good idea to me but it will probably have to be tomorrow. Why don't we all have a seat? Momma, will you sit beside me to the right? Cassie how about you sit to Momma's right and

Shasta, I'd like to have you right beside me. Is that okay?" Shasta nodded, briefly forgetting her family was there. She was crazy in love with this man and had fallen hard. She didn't really think it was possible so soon after her breakup with Seth but she did and it showed every time she looked his way.

Tommy caressed her cheek briefly and turned to Momma. He pulled out her chair and once she was seated, he did the same for Cassie. Shasta was left standing and just as she was about to take her seat, Tommy pulled her chair out for her. She inhaled his cologne. It was such a sweet smell to her nostrils. She closed her eyes just to open them again. This wasn't date night for them. Her family was here and she had to remember that.

"I think we have everything but the drinks. I'm going to head into the kitchen and grab us some glasses and something to drink."

"I poured some lemonade for Momma and Cassie. The glasses are on the kitchen table." Shasta said and Tommy nodded, excusing himself.

"Girl why didn't you prepare me, I could just kick you. Ugh!" Cassie said and Shasta laughed.

"Prepare you for what?"

"You know what. You said he was handsome but that brotha is ***FINE*** and *built.* How do you ...I don't even want to know and this place of his is just too fly. Even Momma was over here stuttering. He made her forget who she was!" Shasta was laughing in earnest now. She had never seen her Momma at a loss for words.

"Well you just stood there letting in flies. Here go one in. Here come another one, wait here come a bee. He wants some honey too. You couldn't close your mouth if a vise grip clamped on it." Momma said and Shasta was in tears. God she missed this. Tommy brought her this and for that, she would forever be thankful.

Chapter 41

"Well I couldn't help it. Like I said, I wasn't prepared. Shasta should've have said something about her man being so fine and charismatic. Not to mention his smell. Momma did you smell him when he touched you? He smelled so good." Momma nodded and looked at Shasta. She had that inquisitive look on her face. Shasta immediately got nervous. She could see Momma's wheels turning in her head.

"Something about him seems so familiar. It's like I've seen him before. Not anywhere specific but...his eyes are so familiar and the way he walks...it's all familiar to me." Shasta sighed inwardly. She knew she couldn't make Tommy reveal to her mother and sister who he was but she hoped he decided to tell them before her mother forced it out of her.

Tommy came back in with the drinks and placed the huge pitcher of lemonade in the center of the table. On a smaller serving tray he had a pitcher of sweet tea and water. He took the lids off the huge silver serving trays and immediately the aroma of delicious scents filled the air. Shasta was overjoyed that Veronica finally done the thing that broke the camel's back. It opened the door for her and gave her a chance to love without restrictions or limits. Her stupidity was the best thing that could have ever happened to her, outside of Tommy.

Tommy unloaded all five of the serving trays carrying Momma's favorites. Smothered pork chops with green peppers and onions in rich brown gravy. Next were the red beans and rice, fried corn and okra. The third server carried candied yams and mountains of corn bread muffins. Server number four buried gifts of black eyed peas with smoked turkey and an extra large serving of macaroni and cheese, enough for six or seven people. The last server had the greatest gift of all, the dessert, a nice fresh homemade peach cobbler.

After Tommy took the third lid off, Momma realized these were all her favorite dishes. She looked at Shasta with a tear in her eye. Shasta nodded but couldn't take credit. This was all Tommy's doing. She just supplied the list and he made sure it all came together. That was why she loved him. Amazing didn't describe him, talented didn't describe him, and reliable didn't describe him. She couldn't find the perfect word to describe him but then she realized she just did. He was perfect, inside and out. She took his hand and he squeezed it, smiling.

“I hope you like everything you see here Momma and before you ask, the only thing here I cooked was the peach cobbler and I think we both know that takes some time to cook.” Everyone laughed and Momma voiced her agreement.

"Everything sure looks and smells delicious, especially the cobbler. You might be making me another one to take back to Virginia when I go home." Momma laughed.

"That wouldn't be a problem. Shall we join hands and say grace." As Tommy said the grace, Shasta looked up and saw her Momma's head was bowed and her eyes were closed as were Cassie's. Everything so far was going perfect, just as perfect as the man holding her hand.

****

Shasta woke up and was shocked not to see Tommy next to her. She thought he was going to take a break from the diner, but then again she realized he wasn't going to leave his family hanging. She got a bright idea to bring Momma and Cassie to the diner so they can get acquainted with Tommy's most proud possession.

"Come on Momma, Cassie let's go to the diner. It should be fun." Shasta opened their door waking both Momma and Cassie up. They all ended up sleeping in the same bed and talked all night, but when Shasta heard Tommy getting out the shower, she returned to their bedroom to sleep peacefully with her man.

"Do we have to get up now? I'm enjoying this big ol' plush bed." Cassie whined.

"Shasta I think that's a great idea. Get up Cassie, you'll be back in that bed tonight. We didn't come to New York City to lay in plush beds."

Cassie rolled her eyes but Momma didn't see her. Momma smiled and headed to the shower. "We will be ready in twenty minutes."

"Fair enough, see you downstairs."

****

Tommy was surprised to see the three of them walk into the diner. He immediately smiled. He missed Shasta and wanted to sleep in with her but he knew Cousin Becky needed assistance.

"I thought it would be a good idea to have Momma and Cassie come down here. I think it's a perfect way for them to get to know your family." Shasta explained.

"No need to explain, Momma has to meet the chef of the place anyways. Before you three have a meal, I want you to come back and meet Cousin Becky." Tommy didn't take no for an answer and Momma wasn't going to refuse to meet the chef. She moved Shasta to the side and walked right behind Tommy, more so because she wanted to suck in his amazing scent.

Cousin Becky was in the middle of mixing some dressing for dinner. She hummed to herself but stopped when she noticed two unfamiliar faces in her area. She right away smiled because she knew exactly who they were.

"It's finally nice to meet you ladies." Cousin Becky said breaking the silence. She reached out for the two ladies to give them a hug. "My, my I see where Shasta gets her good looks from. You must be her sister?" Cousin Becky joked.

Momma smiled, embracing the hug. "Oh I wish! I'm Ms. Brown."

"I'm Cousin Becky, and you are..."

"I'm Cassie, Shasta's older sister." Cassie said after Cousin Becky reached out for a hug.

"Nice to meet you ladies, do you know what you're going to eat for breakfast?"

Momma shook her head and Cassie piped in, "We just got here. By the way the food tasted good last night. I'm certain we will find something amazing to eat for breakfast." Cassie complimented Cousin Becky's cooking.

Cousin Beck blushed. "Well go ahead and have a seat, take a load off and enjoy what I'm about to make ya'll. You all like omelets?" They all shook their heads. "Well I'm going to make you all the best omelets ever!"

"Ladies allow me to take you to your seats." Tommy gestured the ladies back into the diner. He gave them the utensils they needed along with orange juice. "You all just sit tight and enjoy the scenery. Your food will be here shortly."

"He treats you like a queen." Cassie whispered the moment Tommy walked away from them.

"He sure does, I like him...a lot. I don't know what it is but there's something about him." Momma kept her eyes on him.

"What do you ladies want to do after we leave the diner?"

"Why we gotta leave? I want to see what Cousin Becky got going on for dinner. I think she wouldn't mind showing me some ropes in the kitchen."

"Oh Lord." Cassie sighed.

"No I think that's a great idea. Cousin Becky is amazing and she loves teaching people things."

"Yeah, why thank you Shasta." Momma rolled her eyes at Cassie. Before anyone could say anything else their food were placed in front of them. It all looked amazing as Shasta expected.

"Oh I know I'm not going to have a problem eating this." Cassie blurted out.

"This looks great." Shasta gasped. She knew Cousin Becky knew how to hook up an omelet but she didn't expect this. Momma looked at Shasta and raised her eyebrows. "This woman is something else."

Shasta enjoyed every bit of the omelet, and it appeared Cassie and Momma did too. No one said anything during meal time. Shasta sat back in amazement of how much her life had changed. She reminisced on running away from her town with Seth, to sitting at the diner with her family enjoying their meal. She knew things were only going to go up from here.

Chapter 42

Tommy came by the table just as Shawna was clearing the plates. They had just finished their stuffed French toast and Momma was working on her second glass of orange juice. Tommy stood behind Shasta's chair and gently caressed her back with just two fingers. He did it so briefly that when he removed his fingers Shasta almost turned around in her chair but she caught herself.

"I see everyone enjoyed their meal. If there's anything else you want, just tell me. We usually start to get busy in an hour or so but I can help Becky rustle up whatever you like."

"Oh that's fine, we're full but thank you. Breakfast was delicious. I see Cousin Becky and I will have to compare notes. I didn't know they cooked like this in New York. It's like her cooking has a southern appeal to it." Momma sat back in her chair and looked at Tommy. Shasta knew where Momma was leading. Hopefully Tommy did too. She didn't want Momma to talk too much. She wanted Tommy to have the floor. Would he tell her who his father was? He knew her but he didn't know her family and after Veronica, maybe he just felt he couldn't trust anyone so easily.

"My family, most of them are from the south. Becky was taught well. Her mother had her cooking at age nine. She was practically a chef at age sixteen. All she did was cook. It's been her sole job in life and she does do it very well."

"You know, it's just something about you Tommy. I don't know, I can't put my finger on it. You remind me of someone... where's your mother? Is she around? I haven't met her...."

"Momma Brown, both my parents are deceased. My mother passed first, then my father." Tommy paused and sat down, taking the chair next to Shasta, and Shasta inhaled. She took his hand and caressed his knuckles. She looked deep into his eyes and Tommy nodded.

"You may have heard of my father. He had several songs on the radio. They still play many of them today. His name is..."

"Tommy Edwards. He was your daddy...is your daddy. Well I'll be damned." Momma turned to Cassie who looked at Shasta and mouthed, 'why didn't you say something'. Shasta didn't reply. She was just glad it was all out in the open. No more secrets.

"Yes, Tommy Edwards is my father. I didn't know him really. He traveled a lot. My mother went with him often until I came along. She wanted to stay with me then but when I was about twelve, she passed away and I came here to live with her relatives. The house I live in is my fathers. Well, it's mine now and

I've been living there nearly six years." Tommy paused briefly and picked up where he left off.

"As you probably already know, my father died of a brain aneurysm several years ago. It's my wish that one day he will be acknowledged for his success and that one day, I can place that award on my mantle. I know it was something he always wanted. He'd talk to my mother about it often." Shasta smiled and was about to lean in and give Tommy a kiss but something about Momma's expression froze her in her tracks.

"So basically what you're saying is that you're filthy rich." Momma said bluntly.

Shasta blinked twice and stared at her mother. She couldn't believe that just came out of her mouth. She figured Momma would have a problem with her living with Tommy but not this. God please don't let Momma fly from Virginia to New York and start no mess. Things were going just fine until then.

"So you must've invested the money your daddy left you into this diner and bought you that beauty outside. That was smart."

"I think what Momma is trying to say is that she's happy for you, for Shasta. Right Momma?" Cassie tried cleaning up Momma's response, but Shasta didn't know what her Momma meant. It was hard to get a read on Momma. It always had been and as Momma continued to stare at her, Shasta began to wonder just how good an idea it was to uncover this revelation.

****

Tommy could feel Shasta's unease and wanted to set her fears aside. Although he didn't know her family, he knew her. She was what mattered and he didn't like the trembling he felt as he held her hand at his side.

"I'm not filthy rich but I do well for myself. Before my father passed, the diner was already prepped for opening. I dedicated all of my time to working odd jobs and yes saving money to build my dream. I actually have only had that Cadillac close to a year now. I used to drive a Lincoln but I gave that car to one of my relatives in need. My family has always been my support system and have backed me since I came to New York. I did get tangled up with someone who didn't want the best for me but that's all in the past. This beautiful lady sitting next to me is my future, my life." Tommy paused as he reached inside his jacket pocket. Shasta exhaled only to take another deep breath.

Tommy pushed back his chair and got on bended knee. The diner wasn't packed but several customers stopped talking and watched the event unfold. Cousin Becky was called out of the kitchen by Shawna, and Dawn stood behind the counter with a huge smile on her face.

"Since the first moment I saw you at that other diner on 5th street, I was wondering if I would get to see you again. To my surprise, your search for a place to work led you straight to me. I never knew how things would work out learning the situation you were in but that never really mattered. None of it did. My past resolved itself and what you thought was your future turned out to be none-existent. But this here is something I've never known. You filled in so many gaps and holes in my life with your beautiful smile, your comforting touch and your warm embrace. You have brought meaning to my life since the moment you walked through those doors and today I want to ask you to share that life with me." Tommy opened his hand to reveal a green velvet box. Shasta openly cried and had gotten out the chair.

"Yes." She said and one of the women customers spoke out.

"Chile, he ain't even asked yet. Let him ask honey girl. I want to hear him ask." And just like that the rest of the crowd started chanting, 'Ask, ask, ask.' Tommy shook his head but he did want to ask her and since he already knew her answer, he decided to toy with her a bit.

"I don't know guys; I already know her answer so I don't feel like asking now." Tommy saw the shocked look on Shasta's face and laughed outright.

"It was a joke. Just joking." His voice took on a serious tone as he lifted the lid on the small box.

"Shasta Brown, will you wear my ring, love me until I draw my last breath and beyond and take my hand as we work down life's path of mystic adventure. Will you be my wife?" Cassie got up and pushed her toward Tommy. Shasta looked startled and looked back at Momma. Momma too was openly crying. Shasta knew her Momma was happy for her, truly happy. Momma 'mouthed go on now' and Shasta shouted 'Yes'. The diner crowd erupted in applause and whoops of praise. Tommy grabbed her close and kissed her like he had never kissed her before. He placed the three carat princess cut pink diamond on her left ring finger. It was stunning! Shasta smiled through tears of joy as his lips continued their journey connecting again with hers. Her dream had come true. She finally knew what it felt like to ***LOVE.***

Chapter 43

After all the happy mayhem had calmed down, Momma approached Shasta as she knew she would. Shasta knew Momma was happy for her but she still had that look in her eye that made Shasta wary.

"Did you know all along he had money? If you are uniting with this man under false pretenses, it will all blow up in your face. I know I taught you that God don't like ugly."

"No, Momma. I was with Seth when I met Tommy but soon realized he was all wrong for me. The lies, the betrayal, and the broken promises all spelled our doom. I guess we were doomed from the start. Like everyone who knew about us tried to tell me, including you but being with Seth *led* me to Tommy. Tommy could be broke for all I care. It's his heart, mind and soul that I love. Every inch of him is my heart's desire Momma, not his bank account." Momma nodded. She was glad. Her baby girl found what she sought. She had a good man. A man who could take care of her needs and provide all that she wanted. That's all she ever truly wanted for her girls, a good man to love them.

"Well, that's very good to hear. Your Momma didn't raise any leeches. That will turn a man off in a minute and turn a once good man into a heartless bastatrd. It's nice to see you found yourself a good man, a real good provider I might add. Maybe you won't have to work much anymore or not at all."

"Well I'm fine with the at all part but I do feel Shasta's days working inside this diner are over." Tommy said and pulled Shasta close. That wasn't what Shasta wanted to hear. She loved the diner. She loved working with him and seeing his handsome face every day. If she didn't work there, what would she do?

"Tommy, I like it here. Please, I don't want to work any place else." Tommy thought for a minute and thought he had the perfect solution.

"I've been meaning to open up the diner for catering. I'll need someone to create the flyers, do the advertising and order taking...."

"I'll do it!" Shasta was excited and Tommy couldn't resist. He dropped a deep cleansing kiss to her lips, right in front of Momma. After a few seconds, Momma cleared her throat to break the happy couple up.

"Sorry Momma Brown. I couldn't resist kissing my beautiful fiancée. You know, with the business expanding Cousin Becky may need additional help back in the kitchen. Would you like to help her with that?" Shasta looked at Tommy, then at Momma. Tommy was offering her Ma a job. Wow. Would Momma say yes? She hoped so, she really did. Momma didn't make either of them wait long for her answer.

"I guess I need to find me an apron then. Where y'all keep em, in the kitchen?" Tommy laughed and nodded but before Momma made it to the kitchen, Tommy stopped her.

"Momma Brown, my Uncle Titus has a shipping company downtown and he's in need of an organized shipping and receiving manager. The pay is good. Maybe your son- in-law might be interested. I believe it starts at $4 an hour but he and Uncle Titus can work out the details if he shows an interest and since my fiancée's old job is vacant, it's Cassie's if she wants it." Shasta watched her Momma's eyes light with delight as she ran into the kitchen.

Shasta was beyond happy. Tommy had come into her life at the perfect time and turned it right side up. He'd given her so much in such a short time. The pain she once felt was forgotten. The joy she felt now ran so deep that it almost hurt but it was a welcoming pain from the depths of her soul. This love was pure and ***untainted.***

****

Shasta had too much excitement for one day, she was glad when Cassie asked to go back to the house. Momma wasn't leaving any time soon and assured the girls she'd be fine at the diner with Cousin Becky. Those two ladies hit it off quickly. It amazed her watching the two women in the kitchen making amazing meals. She wanted to break down and cry but then too much attention would be on her.

"Come on Shasta, you ready?" Cassie interrupted her thoughts.

"Yeah."

"I'm so excited. As soon as I get to the house I'm going to call the hubby and tell him to take the next flight up. Then Momma...well Momma can sell the house, she can make a profit off of that and settle right here in New York! Isn't this great, we all are going to be under one roof living the life!"

Shasta smiled, observing Cassie's happiness. She was extremely happy, nothing could put her down.

"Yes, all under one roof like the old days. The good news is Momma's good relationship with Tommy and his family. For a second there I thought things were going to go sour."

"I bet you did. I was a bit scared for a second too." Cassie confessed. "The look on Momma's face was priceless, it...it was indescribable."

"It sure was and my man handled it smoothly."

"You mean your fiancé, you better claim it now girl. You's gonna be married soon! So after I make a phone call to the hubby we got some wedding planning to do."

"I completely forgot about that. I think I'm going to get a wedding coordinator. With Tommy needing help setting up the diner for catering, I know I'm going to have a hard time doing things on my own."

"That makes a lot of sense, that slipped my mind. I remember when I got married things were so difficult to do on my own. I prayed I could afford a wedding coordinator and couldn't."

"I know. I remember when you sat in Momma's living room and cried. I was in the middle of making the party favors." Both the girls burst into laughter as Shasta pulled up to the front of the house.

"Give me about an hour and I we'll start looking for wedding planners. We can look in the newspaper. I know we will find something there."

"Yes and afterwards we can go to a bridal shop and try some dresses on."

"I think you should wait for Momma to do that right?" Cassie made a face.

"I guess you're right."

Cassie ran to the phone and made her phone call. At that moment Shasta's thoughts went to her best friend. She missed Laquenta. Just the thought of her name made her tear up. She hated the way they ended things. It wasn't good, and she knew besides Momma and Cassie, she had to have Laquenta witness her happiness. She was all about being happy, besides she wanted to know what she was up to. Maybe she could make an offer to come up to New York, and possibly her family too.

"I'm going to change my clothes Shasta," Cassie yelled after she got off the phone. "Then we can start with the wedding plans." Her voice became louder as she walked closer to Shasta.

"Okay, that's fine. I will be in the kitchen, just come down here once you're ready." Cassie disappeared upstairs as Shasta stared at the phone. She picked it up, dialed Laquenta's phone number and prayed their conversation would end in laughter.

****

"You think I would ever miss out on an opportunity to go to New York City?" Laquenta shouted after embracing Shasta with a hug. "No, not one bit."

"It's been so long, I missed you so much. There's so much I need to catch you up on." Shasta took Laquenta's carryon bag as they made their way to the baggage claim. Shasta was ecstatic. Her phone call a week ago made this reunion happen.

"Look I'm so glad you left Seth. I know I wasn't the best person to give you advice especially after my little mishap."

"Yeah, I'm sorry about that. Have you ran into him?"

"Nope, and don't plan on it neither. Girl after you left with Seth things went bananas."

"I know my Momma told me they did, as well as Cassie. "

"Well shoot I don't want to go back. Heck if I could make a living up here and bring my family, that's what I'd do! Ain't nothin' in Virginia, just a bunch of old white hags who ain't givin' any opportunities. Heck I want to live the wealthy life. I want to be able to walk up in that store and say...hey...I want everything in here pronto!" Laquenta joked.

Shasta laughed. She sure missed her friend. She knew Laquenta was crazy but she needed to be around that. Laquenta missed out on way too much and Shasta wasn't going to allow her to miss out on anything else.

"So this Tommy guy, how is he?" Laquenta battered her eyes as they got into the car.

"He's amazing, breathtaking, a fresh new start."

"You can say that again." Laquenta said looking at her ring. "So I take it a wedding is going to be soon?"

"Yes, sooner than I suppose. I have to get to it. I need a dress, a venue, a church...heck my man's place is so big we don't need to go anywhere but in the backyard. But I do need a preacher, Momma ain't gonna have me down in no court house saying I do! She'd slap me silly and ask questions later." Shasta scoffed.

"Oh I know Momma don't play any games." Laquenta laughed.

Shasta shook her head. "So you want to go past the diner to meet Tommy."

"Sure, my Momma always told me it's important to meet the man of the house before you walk *in* his house...if you catch my drift."

"Oh I caught it alright. Sit tight we're only a few blocks away."

Laquenta didn't care how many blocks away they were, her eyes gazed on the tall buildings and the people walking in the city. "All these people walking around here like it's nothing."

"They got somewhere to be." Shasta said maneuvering the big, beautiful car.

"I never seen this many people in my life, this is insane." Laquenta gasped. "Shoot, I thought the supermarkets were packed, that ain't got nothing on this."

"Oh and believe me, it takes some getting used to."

"I don't know Shasta." Laquenta didn't take her eyes off the window. It humored Shasta because of the reaction everyone had once they arrived to New York City. It was a reminder of when she first arrived. She knew after Laquenta got settled she'd be ready to hit the town.

Chapter 44

Laquenta eyes widened, starring at Tommy. Shasta closed her mouth and snapped her fingers to snap her back to reality. “Laquenta...did you hear me?”

“Huh...no...wait, what?” She smiled at Tommy and he stook his hand out for her to shake and she shook it repeatedly. “It’s a pleasure to meet you.”

“Thanks, I feel the same way.” Tommy smiled. Laquenta nodded and looked around the diner. “This place is nice. I love what you did with it.” Laquenta said as if she knew Tommy on a personal level.

“Thank you, I’ve came a long way with it. It wasn’t easy but I managed to get it done.”

“That’s nice.” Laquenta replied, still staring at Tommy's handsome face.

“Laquenta...is that you?” Momma asked as she tilted her head behind the wall.

“Hey Momma, yeah it’s me.” Laquenta laughed. “What you doing back there?”

“Working, come on over here and give me a hug. I want you to meet Cousin Becky,” Momma was excited to see a familiar face, it made her feel comfortable knowing Shasta had support now.

"This is Cousin Becky," Laquenta shook her hand and smiled. "Nice to meet you,"

"The pleasure is all mine sweetheart. Did you eat on the plane?"

"Not really, I mean they gave out some peanuts and soda but I'm still hungry." She rubbed her stomach looking around in the back. She smelled sweet potato pies, apple and cherry pie. "It smells great in here." Laquenta complimented. She turned her head and noticed Shasta talking to Tommy. They both looked happy and she was very happy to witness it.

****

The date was set for an April wedding. Shasta didn't have much time so she, Cassie, and Laquenta got the guest list, the food list, and the flower arrangements together quickly. She asked Cassie to stand up for her and Laquenta, Shawna, Dawn and Antoinette would be her bridesmaids. Tommy had a few cousins who came around the diner who would be his groomsmen. Cousin Becky and Momma would both light the candles at the wedding. Cousin Becky's minister, Reverend James R. Tisdale would officiate the wedding.

Everything was all set but the dress. Tommy wanted her to pick something out at Saks Fifth Avenue but Shasta wanted to save some money and found a cute boutique only a few blocks away that was more reasonably priced. She liked the dresses there and picked out two different gowns. She knew she had to make a decision soon, so she and Cassie would drive there today for her to make a decision.

"Hey baby. Momma needs to talk to you for a minute." Shasta was deep in thought; she didn't hear Momma walk up. She sat at the kitchen table going over catalog marketing ideas for the restaurant's catering service.

"Sure Momma. I'll be leaving in a little bit. Cassie and I are going to pick a dress today. I really don't have a choice. The wedding is just three weeks away now."

"I know sweetheart, I know. I was really glad to hear that you will be getting married in a church. I've only been to Mt. Sinai once but it seems like a very nice church and pastor Tisdale can preach. He brought an uplifting sermon when I went a few Sunday's ago that had me thinking..." Shasta pushed her chair back and stood up. There Momma went making her nervous again. What did she mean the sermon had her thinking?

"Now hold on. I can see the wheels turning in that pretty little head of yours. I got to say this though honey chile. I was wrong. I was wrong for the way I reacted when I learned you were seeing that white boy. I had a lot of anger still from losing your father and you mixing up with one of them didn't help any. I should have tried to make you see from a different angle. I should've been more patient..."

"Momma, none of that matters now. We're all past that and..." Momma cut her off by putting a finger to her mouth.

"Let me finish chile. You were always so anxious. After that sermon I thought I'd caught the Holy Ghost but the Holy Ghost wasn't what followed me home that afternoon, it was my guilt. I sat here in this very kitchen and released that river of tears. I never let myself cry for you. They just came and wouldn't stop and that's when he found me."

"Reverend Tisdale came here?" Shasta was confused and it clearly shown on her face.

"No, Tommy found me. He comforted me and told me things about life I won't soon forget. What he told me cleansed my soul and I realized that instead of being mad that you took off with that boy, I should be happy because when you left, it led you here to that wonderful man. He's worthy of you honey girl and you are of him. I'm so damn happy for you." Shasta hugged her Momma and they both cried tears of joy. They embraced for a while then her Momma pulled away.

"And that all just leads me to my next acknowledgement, baby. Your sister and I are moving out." At Shasta's gasp, Momma continued on.

"Chile you will be a newlywed real soon. We can't be staying here when you get back from your honeymoon from the Virgin Islands. I know how you honeymooners can get and I don't want to walk in on anything by accident." Shasta smiled. She would miss Momma but she wanted some alone time with Tommy. They had been leaving the restaurant late, heading home to make sweet love after Cassie and Momma settled in for the night.

"Momma where will you go? There's the guest house in the back..."

"Oh ,no. It's all taken care of. That Uncle Titus sure is something else. Yes he is. He found this duplex not ten minutes from here. It's huge! Cassie's gonna take the upstairs. It's a three bedroom, two bath and I'm getting the bottom. It's a huge two bedroom with one bath and a sitting room. I got the enclosed porch too." Shasta smiled again. Her Momma was happy and had that gleam she had in her eye when she mentioned Uncle Titus, it was too cute.

"See honey chile, we all can have everything we ever dreamed of because of you. It's all because of you baby. Laquenta is moving in with Shawna temporarily until she starts work at the grocery store and another apartment opens up. She'll just be bagging right now but she'll work her way up. You don't worry about us. We'll be just fine. Here comes Cassie now. You go get that dress and when you're ready to walk down that aisle I'll be right there in the front row watching you." Momma took off and Shasta silently sent up a prayer to God thanking Him for making her dreams come true.

Chapter 45

The day had finally arrived. Shasta's nerves took over her. It had a lot to do with the wedding day jitters but it also had to do with the news she had to deliver to Tommy. The night before had been crazy. Momma and Cassie had gotten settled into their new place and Laquenta had caught a cab to the house. Shasta wasn't feeling well and went to splash some water on her face when Laquenta came to stand next to her. Her perfume made Shasta instantly nauseous and Shasta threw up right there in the sink.

Laquenta was cleaning the sink when another bout hit Shasta head on. She made it to the trash can this time and Laquenta quickly poured her some water.

"Girl, you okay. You're not coming down with anything are you? Tomorrow's your wedding day. You need to see the doctor or something?"

"No, I think it's your perfume or something. I must be allergic to it." Shasta replied but really didn't think that was the problem.

"Okay, why don't you go lay down. I'll call the cab place and leave once Tommy comes back. He's still out with the fellas having a drink, right?" Shasta nodded but felt faint. She took two steps from the kitchen and fainted.

That prompted Laquenta to call a cab immediately and they headed to the hospital. Shasta was there only an hour but it seemed like an eternity. She slept in the big house and Tommy slept in the guest house as they planned. She got up and showered and put her hair up. She talked very little to her sister and Momma and everyone just thought it was pre-wedding jitters. It was going on noon and the wedding was to start at two. Shasta couldn't take the anticipation anymore and raced down to the guest house with nothing on but her blue, silk robe. Her sister tried to stop her but her Momma let her go.

She found Tommy looking like a greek model in his tuxedo. His back was to her when she opened the door but sensing her presence, he turned around.

"Baby, what are you doing here? Why aren't you dressed? It's almost noon. You should be getting ready..."

"I'm pregnant Tommy. I found out last night when you were out with the fellas. Laquenta took me to the hospital in a cab. I thought I had the flu or something but the doctor said I'm pregnant. I'm ten weeks." Shasta could feel the sting of tears in the back of her eyelids. She knew the baby was Tommy's but would he believe it was his? It had been months since she and Seth had slept together. They hadn't been intimate for several weeks, even before she learned of his infidelity but would Tommy believe that she was only ten weeks pregnant? They had been official for just over three months now. She had agonized all night over this and she knew what another woman would do, what a woman like Veronica would do and she vowed to not be like her. She wanted this man and she wanted honesty, something Seth never gave her. Tommy deserved her honesty, along with her love. She knew she had to tell him, she had to give him a choice.

"Tommy, I know this baby is yours. It can only be yours. Seth and I never had a tenth of the passion that we share. We hadn't been intimate for a long time, long before we got together. He didn't need me anymore. He had Emily...Shannon or whatever she was calling herself..."

"Enough. I heard enough." Shasta inhaled deeply. She was beyond nervous now. She was damn near in a panic. She couldn't lose Tommy now. She just couldn't. She loved him so but if he didn't feel he could trust her, where did that leave them? He had been through the ringer with Veronica. Would he want to chance it with her learning what she just told him?

When Tommy turned around, Shasta finally exhaled. She saw love and adoration in his eyes. Something she thought she may never see again.

"Enough talk about that dumb fool and his tramp. We have a wedding to get to. I know this baby is mine...even if it were his; I'd raise it as mine because of you Shasta. This baby... if you say it's mine, then it is. I'm not mistaking you for anyone else. I know exactly who you are and by now I think you'd know who I am as well. I'm the man who loves you, all of you. From that peanut head of yours to the tips of your pretty little toes. Now we're gonna be a family. I'm gonna be a daddy and you're gonna be the best momma there is. I'm sure of it because our love isn't tainted. It's pure, it's magnificent and perfect. Just like you." Shasta's whole heart smiled and she ran to him. Tommy picked her up and set her down. He lowered his head and they kissed passionately, for a moment forgetting they had a wedding to start.

"Ahem, sorry to have to break this up but everyone's waiting for the bride." Laquenta said, causing Shasta to slowly pull away from Tommy. Tommy brushed his lips once more to hers before letting her go. He leaned down and whispered, 'see you in an hour, my love.' Shasta practically ran from the guesthouse, anxious to start her new life with the love of her life.

****

Shasta beamed with happiness as Reverend Tisdale pronounced them man and wife. She had walked down the isle of the church on a bed of petaled red roses. Derek gave her away and both Momma and Cousin Becky lit their unity candles to seal the blessed union. When Tommy leaned in close to kiss his bride, Shasta had to remember that they were in a church full of friends and family and tried not to show out.

As their family and friends threw rice at them and shouted out their well wishes of prosperity and happiness, Shasta finally realized she found what Tommy had told her all along that could be theirs. She had found her ***untainted love***.

Study Guide Questions

1. Shasta was eager to find love and from the moment she met Seth, she knew he was the one. Where did Seth take her on their first date and how did she get there?

2. Shasta had a great friendship with Laquenta and Laquenta covered for her often. When was the first time Laquenta covered for Shasta and when was the last time?

3. Shasta and Seth's relationship was forbidden to many of the towns folk in Virginia, thus the reason for them sneaking around. Name some of the places they met up to sneak in some 'quality' time.

4. Seth worked at his family owned car wash and Shasta worked at the discount store but Shasta's job was very difficult on so many levels. Name some of the problems she encountered at the discount store and think about what you would've done differently it you faced the same issues at your work place.(Validate and discuss)

5. Shasta got suspended from work which probably came as no surprise but when she returned to work, she had a scheme of her own cooked up compliments of her good friend

Laquenta. Discuss the scheme they set in motion to frame Emily.

6. Shasta got a promotion and was practically running the store but soon the towns folks learned of her and Seth's relationship and she knew her days of working at the discount store were numbered. What happened that lead to Shasta abandoning her new position and her and Laquenta falling out? Soon after the falling out with her friend, Shasta and Seth fled to the cabin. They were on the go and for good reason. The town folks wanted her head but Seth was never in any real danger. Shasta had to always stay hidden when she was alone with Seth. Name some of the places Seth had her hide when she was at the cabin and why.

7. When Shasta and Seth fled to New York, Shasta wanted to leave her old life behind. Part of that meant her family. As she sat eating her meal with Seth in the first diner, a news broadcast came on the TV and she heard her Ma speak on the tragedies that she had caused. Was her mother right in blaming her for all that happened *after* she left?

8. Seth had gotten a job practically the moment his feet hit the pavement in New York but for Shasta, it wasn't that easy. Her tired feet and her thirst from searching for work led her

straight to Sweet Daddy Tommy's doorstep. When Shasta sat down in the diner, she was appreciative of the sweet smells and the diner's ambiance but what made her come back there the next day?

9. Shasta was offered a job and she took it but before long, she and Seth began having problems. What was their first real blow up about?

10. Tommy fascinated Shasta and he was just as fascinated by her but he had one major distraction that wouldn't go away. **Veronica.** She would come and go as she did many times in his life but he couldn't seem to let go. What was Veronica's hold on him and how did Shasta find out?

11. When Shasta and Seth moved into the small apartment, things really went south and never went back north. Discuss some of the things Shasta learned/discovered that sealed their fate and eventually caused her to leave Seth.

12. When Shasta left Seth, she immediately wanted Tommy's big, broad shoulders to cry on. She had wanted him for a long time and knew he wanted her but Tommy didn't immediately respond the way she wanted him to. What was his reasoning behind it?

13. Cousin Becky was both Tommy and Shasta's voice of reason and Shasta went to Cousin Becky often for advice. What advice did she give to Shasta when Shasta asked her about how to get to Tommy?

14. Once Shasta and Tommy got together, it was like nothing Shasta had ever felt before. She felt loved and cherished, like she truly belonged. Her man rocked her world and not just in the bedroom either. She was no longer hiding from anyone or anything. She was free to love openly but she still missed her family. When Tommy realized this was something she longed for, he wanted to appease her. What seven words did he whisper in her ear as she talked to her mother on the phone?

15. Shasta's dreams were fulfilled and she couldn't be happier with her life. Momma, Cassie and Laquenta had all flown in for her big day but just hours before her wedding, she was a complete nervous wreck. What had she learned just the night before that made her feel like love and happiness might not be hers to take afterall? Why would this upset her? What was Tommy's response when she told him?

16. How did this novel measure up to some of the most recent interracial romance novels that you've read?

About The Author

Author Jamie Rockymore was born in Pittsburgh, Pennsylvania. She went to Clarion University of Pennsylvania and graduated with a B.A Degree. During her senior year of college she discovered her love for writing novels. After writing her book she started a website: JamieRockymore.com, there she obtain readers and attraction from other publishing companies. Her first book that gained attention was *Simply Unique Short Stories,* with the response from different readers; Author Jamie Rockymore published her first novel *Class in Session.* In addition to that she published *It's Better to Lie.* She has a few more novels to publish within the year. Author Jamie Rockymore can be reached on her website JamieRockymore.com, Twitter @JamieRockymore, or on Facebook at AuthorJamieRockymore.

About The Author

Madeline began reading romance novels at an early age. Her intense love of the written word led her to her eventual goal of becoming a published author. After graduating from high school, Madeline served her country for three years as a flight specialist in the U.S. Military. While there she met and married the love of her life. After leaving the service with an honorable discharge, she moved back to her hometown of Toledo, Ohio. Madeline has participated in several literary conferences and book signings, including her first one which was a joint session with renown author Victoria Christopher Murray. Today Madeline resides in Toledo and enjoys the support of her family, friends, colleagues and her loving husband Johnnie. Madeline feels Mr.& Mrs. Love Jones is her best selling novel. You can check out Madeline's other works on amazon.com and follow her on Twitter @madeline419. Friend her on Facebook @Author Madeline Hampton.

www.ingramcontent.com/pod-product-compliance
Lightning Source LLC
LaVergne TN
LVHW051451080426
835509LV00017B/1739

* 9 7 8 0 6 1 5 9 7 1 9 2 6 *